Stories I Lived to Tell
_____

STORiES I Lived to Tell

AN APPALACHIAN MEMOIR

GARY CARDEN

EDITED BY NEAL HUTCHESON

THE UNIVERSITY OF NORTH CAROLINA PRESS

Chapel Hill

© 2024 Gary Carden

© 2024 introduction Neal Hutcheson

All photographs courtesy of the author.

All rights reserved

Designed by Jamison Cockerham
Set in Scala, Sentinel, and Poplar
by Jamie McKee, MacKey Composition

Manufactured in the United States of America

Cover art by Caitlin Cary, 2023.

Complete Library of Congress Cataloging-in-Publication Data for this title is available at https://lccn.loc.gov/2024020848.

ISBN 978-1-4696-8156-6 (cloth: alk. paper)
ISBN 978-1-4696-8157-3 (pbk.: alk. paper)
ISBN 978-1-4696-8158-0 (epub)
ISBN 978-1-4696-8159-7 (pdf)

for Dot

Contents

Acknowledgments ix
Introduction: Gary Carden, Storyteller xi

Mother's Visit 3
Memory 6
Dear Miss Sadie 7
Mason Jars in the Flood 9
The Raindrop Waltz 13
The Drowned Babe 15
Jack Frost 18
Uncle Albert 21
Charlie's Funny Books 22
Bad Blood 26
Abner, the Wild Monkey of the Smokies 28
Grandfather's New Dodge Pickup 31
The Green Fly Café 33
Gall Lake 37
Jiggs, My Little Red Rooster 40
Ode to the Sylva Coffee Shop 43

Things Have Been Bad, But... 44

The Pink Radio 47

Billy Condon 50

Sadie Womack 53

Booger 55

My Grandfather and Jesse James 59

Gun Trade 62

Mountain Water as Religion 72

Coffins in the Flood 73

The Hanging of Bayless Henderson 76

Blow the Tannery Whistle! 80

Tiny 84

Christmas in Cowee 88

The Rhodes Cove Grinch 91

The *Lucky Strike Hit Parade* 93

Dr. Blosser's Cigarettes 96

The Kingdom of the Happy Land 99

Love's Field 105

Outside, Looking In 106

The Green Tsunami 109

Valentino 112

Midnight on Freeze Hill 114

The Bootlegger's Turn 116

The Hoyle House 120

Uncle Frank 123

Vernon Cope 125

What This House Remembers 127

Image gallery follows page 64

Acknowledgments

I wish to acknowledge my debt to Dot Jackson, an honored author who has been called "the true voice of Appalachia." For many years, she shared the front-page columns in the *Charlotte Observer* where she paid homage to the folkways and culture of these mountains. Her promotion of my first book, *Mason Jars in the Flood*, resulted in it receiving the Appalachian Book of the Year Award in 2001. Her encouragement led to the writing and production of all of my plays; indeed, she was the primary source for *The Prince of Dark Corners*, since she was steeped in the story of the outlaw Lewis Redmond. Near the end of her life, she finally submitted her novel, *Refuge*, for publication. Of course, it was a brilliant work that captured the magic and the beauty of Appalachia. Bless you, Dot!

I have one other heartfelt acknowledgment. When I was seventeen, I met a green-eyed, red-headed beauty named Jo Anne Patterson, and although our lives went separate ways, Jo Anne remained my friend for life. Storytelling proved to be a risky way to make a living. It became even more difficult when, at thirty, I became "profoundly deaf." Jo Anne took me to Chapel Hill and supervised a cochlear implant. When I was fifty and was employed as a storyteller in the elder hostels in my region, my car caught on fire and burned on Cowee Mountain. I was deprived of transportation and denied assistance by my own family, but Jo Anne bought a car and left it in my driveway. When my mother was dying in Tennessee, she asked me to come see her, for she had an explanation for why she had abandoned me. Jo Anne took me to Tennessee, and the results altered my life. So, here are three reasons (and all is not accounted) that explain why I survived as a storyteller and why this book has become a reality. Thank you, Jo Anne!

Introduction: Gary Carden, Storyteller

By Neal Hutcheson

The world of his childhood was literally alive with
unseen meaning and connections and miracles;
even the stones had lives and stories.

DAN SIMMONS, *BLACK HILLS*

Gary turns eighty-nine this winter. He lives in an old house that you will learn much more about in this book. He is alone there, except for the abundant company of his housecat, raccoons (outside, usually), memories, and ghosts. The birds stay busy around the house and the flora never stops. He is surviving, with the yeoman's service of a soapstone wood stove, a motorized wheelchair, and a cochlear implant.

I don't need to tell you Gary's story. He is about to do that himself. But I would like to say a little more about the house that he haunts in life, and—if the universe is as interesting as it seems—will continue to haunt long after the spirit exits the body. The old farmhouse in Rhodes Cove where Gary was raised by his grandparents is the setting of my documentary *Storyteller*. In hindsight, I notice in the film an impulse to preserve this privileged space, filming it from every direction and angle, then reassembling it in another medium. It's one of those habitations that became an externalization of the inhabitant. It is not just a *reflection* of the personality of the person within. Somehow, it *is* the person within.

The porch, in particular, is the stage on which the narrative of Gary's life played out. There on those worn boards is where his mother left him when he was two years old, shortly after his father's murder, to be raised by his grandparents according to the customs of an earlier generation. It is where Gary played, grew, gardened, painted, fed thousands of hummingbirds, read a million books, and told stories to friends and visitors beyond counting. The myths, tall tales, folklore, and history of the region have all been revived there and found company with one another.

In my documentary, filmed over nearly twenty-five years, the house visibly decays, a suitable analogue of other elements in the film—the storyteller in question and the arc of life. It's an outpost from which Gary has viewed a changing world over (nearly) nine decades, made sense of it through narrative, adapted, and survived. It is also a place of power where he himself has reassembled the world and the vibrant culture he knew in his early days, bringing it back to life in service to the community, not to tell them who they were but to remind them who they are. This storytelling business is not an exercise in nostalgia, it is essential.

GARY HAS MET SERIOUS CHALLENGES to his health over the years, beginning in childhood, and prevailed. Recent years have taken a toll on his body, but his mind and natural talents remain remarkable. I recently drove him to a small healthcare facility deep in a Jackson County holler, where he had been invited to tell stories in the community room and was startled by the number of people who came to see and hear him. He had been making light conversation with the folks in the first row of chairs, and when he was ready to begin there was no signal or cue but a palpable shift in the room as attention was drawn forward. He began to set the stage. The room, walls, and ceiling were gone in short order, and we were welcomed to his space, an Appalachian community brought forward eight decades from the past. Birds sang. Marbles clicked in the dust of the trail that led into the cove. The pages of a "funny book" rustled. And drifting in from somewhere in the far distance, from the direction of the Balsam Mountains, muted string music, and . . . was that a gunshot? With a gathering of rapt listeners in the cup of his hand, he is a marvel, absolutely undiminished.

Once, in decrying the professional storyteller types (suspenders and bow ties, funny hats) who bring crisply timed anecdotes with pat biblical morals to heritage festivals, Gary told me, "I never know what I'm going to say until I say it. I just open my mouth and talk. And *that's* storytelling." And so it was. The morning before the event, while sharing his invariable breakfast of eggs, sausage patties, and coffee, Gary said, "What do you think I should talk about today?" "The Night They Buried Traveler," I suggested. Or, what about Miss Tiny and her cats? He lost interest in my suggestions and the conversation drifted other places—a movie he had seen recently, or the day's news. It was a phenomenon I had witnessed many times before—Gary was not troubled by the fact that he would soon be in front of an expectant audience, all eyes upon him . . . and he hadn't planned anything to say.

When the time came, he just started talking. And then, there it was, an audience taken out of their lives for a little while, masterfully guided. Themes emerged, delineating a powerful sense of place and the complications of family, and then—as if this convoluted tale had been meticulously prepared in a laboratory, mapped out over several weeks using a large erase board, colored yarn, photos, and cutouts—all of the threads came together in a resounding conclusion that brought murmurs of appreciation and then, applause.

The stories collected here, in another medium, can't replicate the experience of hearing Gary tell stories extemporaneously, but they do capture and preserve a lot of the raw material from which Gary draws in those moments. The stories all originated individually, but they work together beautifully, conspiring to bring an Appalachian community intact from the first half of the twentieth century into the present. If the particulars occasionally press the limits of credulity, need it be said that embellishment goes with the territory? "There is a thing about storytelling," Gary once said. "Sometimes you have to tell a truth more significant than the facts."

YOUNG GARY NEIL CARDEN was brought up in a place where expressive language, storytelling, and hard truths were inescapable, flowing through the branches and hollers of the region like its life's blood. He was an abnormally sensitive child and the fertile cultural climate of Jackson County shaped him and prepared him for a particular fate. Indeed, the trajectory of Gary's life has a narrative grace all its own, from a dangerously imaginative towheaded boy, viewed with grave concern and misgivings by those entrusted with his care, to a *tradition bearer*. "Oh my," he will say, discomfited by sanction and suspicious of the implication that he has become allied to any kind of institution.

His reservations notwithstanding, recent years have inflicted all manner of recognition upon him, from an honorary doctorate (Western Carolina University) to the North Carolina Award (the Old North State's highest civilian honor), and a host of other prestigious acknowledgments in between. A feature-length documentary about him has just premiered, and now this treasury of his work. How will he bear it, I wonder?

IN TRUTH, GARY HAS BEEN FORCED to carry far more than anyone ought. The laurels that recent years have stacked on his brow may be some consolation, but in the end the telling of stories has been the only way forward for him, a lifeline, a negotiation with reality and a means of survival. No one asked if he'd liked to do it. No one suggested it would be a good career. In fact, he was actively discouraged by (nearly) every adult and authority figure in his life. And the first time he told stories professionally, he returned home to discover an anonymous note on his porch in carefully penned capital letters. It read, OUR CULTURE WAS BUILT ON IGNORANCE AND SUPERSTITION LET IT DIE. Gary did not heed the admonishment, but it must have stunned him. He pinned the note to the wall, where it remains today for his perpetual contemplation.

The stories herein are quilted into a memoir that, through the experiences of the author, illuminate a time and place in Appalachia and highlight the complications of change, adaptation, and loss in the region. It is a story he is uniquely qualified to tell. His personal history opened with a tragedy that invested his life with a sense of abandonment and loss from before he could speak—the sort of crucible in which storytellers are made, according to the psychoanalyst Clarissa Pinkola Estés. It is hard to miss the fact that his stories revisit his father's death and the events that led to his abandonment on his grandparents' porch time and time again, perpetually seeking to give order and reason and merit to a chaotic and unstructured series of events that left him feeling forever unwanted in the world. . . . But that scene keeps giving way to others that open up the bright dimensions of his life and the life of the community. Whatever challenges and insults were heaped upon him in childhood, his stories speak to an abiding regard for the cultural richness of the world he knew back then. He conjures it up through cathead biscuits and cats-eye marbles, Mason jars and mandolins, primarily through his own childhood experiences but also through the tales that circulated in the region, stories that transported him and fired his young imagination. His affection for those days, antecedent of "street lights and pavement," is neither sentimental nor nostalgic in intent. In restoring his childhood community to life, replete with characters that say and do amazing, surprising things, he is not only telling us what the community *was* but reminding us what it *is*. There is darkness and light, sunshine and grit, cornfields and cow shit, folly, disappointment, and awe. There are failed marriages, wrecked vehicles, bullies, bullets, and blood. In the end, this is not a version of midcentury mountain life that makes for children's literature, but it is unmistakably real. Together his stories collaborate on a depiction of Appalachian culture that is both dignified *and* honest, something that has been all too rare in our nation's history.

In one interview, made to support our television production of his play *The Prince of Dark Corners,* Gary remarked, "Some of the early people that came in here, one of them wrote a book about mountain people and the title of it, I love! It was *A Strange and Most Peculiar People.* Yes! Well, why are we strange and most peculiar? I want my characters to explain that. Perhaps when they get through, it is my hope that we are no longer strange and peculiar, that we're very much a part of the human race."

I FIRST MET GARY at the turn of the century, while working in western North Carolina on a documentary called *Mountain Talk*. I had recently completed a series of audio recordings and a short film with the legendary poet-publisher Jonathan Williams of Highlands, and so I called Jonathan for advice on a documentary about Southern Appalachian language. He told me one thing, find Gary Carden. As it happened, I already knew the name by way of a "found poem" that Williams had produced from a bit of conversation reported to him from the Coffee Shop in Sylva:

> whatzit you readin' carden
> jonathan williams izat the
> funny feller you must
> be thinking of winters

hell yes down to
20 degrees this morning

I made a couple of embarrassing and unsuccessful attempts to talk to Gary on the phone (Gary is deaf and the brief conversations we had were much like Williams's poem) and then I took a chance and just showed up at his house in Sylva. I found Gary in the sunlight on the side porch, taking a break from painting, reading *Walking on Ice*, a memoir by German filmmaker Werner Herzog. I was fanatical about Herzog at the time. Gary told me, "He's my favorite filmmaker." I said, "Mine too!" And we've been thick as thieves ever since.

While making *Mountain Talk,* Gary not only gave me an interview that anchored the film but a couch to sleep on while I was in the area—an arrangement that would support numerous other documentaries and television productions over the years, including a PBS project on ballad-singer Mary Jane Queen and her musical family, several adaptations of Gary's plays based on regional folklore and history, and a couple of humble but now infamous documentaries I made about the moonshiner Popcorn Sutton. And we finally premiered *Storyteller*, the documentary on Gary himself, on the tail end of an arc that began almost twenty-five years ago.

When I tumbled unexpectedly into the rabbit hole of Appalachian culture, Gary proved an essential guide and consultant. He has consistently and tirelessly challenged and complicated the public's assumptions about mountain people in his stories, dramatic works, and newspaper columns. Born and raised in the heart of Southern Appalachia, steeped in the region's culture, he himself defies simplistic, popular, and stereotypical depictions of mountain people as provincial and ignorant of the world outside the region. He has an encyclopedic knowledge of foreign film and an extensive appetite for all manner of books and culture, whether "books" means Cormac McCarthy, Thomas Wolfe, or Robert Crumb, and whether "culture" means popular, esoteric, underground, or folk. He engages with any tale that carries forward the spark and play of our humanity, whether it takes the form of folklore or "funny books." In his view, the delight of the tale, found anywhere from *Sub-mariner* to *Sergeant Preston of the Yukon*, is often all that's required for that noble task.

WORKING ON THE *Storyteller* documentary, I came to see storytelling as a way to come to terms with the insults and disappointments and confusions of life, as well as to contextualize its rewards. In one part of the film, Gary explains, "Anytime you're dealing with reality, you're dealing with chaos. And the whole purpose of an artist is to take the isolated little pieces of chaos and connect them with little bridges, and . . . it's an artifice, it's a fake. You created that order . . . but it makes it make sense." Or, as Joan Didion wrote, "We tell ourselves stories in order to live."

Not all of the neighbors who visited his grandparents' house (where Gary was raised) saw it that way. "I was constantly telling people things they didn't want to hear," he said. At six or so years old, he was recounting the travails of Lassie when his grandfather's friend stopped him short with a rebuke he never forgot: "Son, that ain't nothing but *shadows on the wall*." His grandfather often referred to him as a "quare young'en," and many of his teachers intervened to tell his grandmother, whom he called "Momma," that Gary Neil couldn't distinguish fantasy from reality. "She was wrong about that," Gary says. "I knew the difference, I just preferred one to the other."

Today, the storyteller in consideration lives comfortably in the realm of memory and folklore and stories a large part of the time, and somewhat uncomfortably outside of that realm the rest of the time. Who is to say, then, which side of the line is the best to call reality? Whether speaking of the ghosts that roam his house in liminal moments, or the dim mirage of present-day Sylva that wavers in his vision like vapor over a robust 1940s and 1950s Appalachian town, Gary often returns to Tennyson's lines on Camelot:

> ... the city is built
> To music, therefore never built at all,
> And therefore built for ever.

We are now not only in the realm of biography but identity, of imaginative memory at the heart of a community. It is a privileged space, to which the price of access is only our attention.

Hush now. The storyteller is about to begin.

Stories I Lived to Tell

Kind hearts, let me tell you a story...

Mother's Visit

Well, kind hearts, I remember that it was summer and I was probably seventeen and school was out, and I spent most of my time in my bedroom with my comic books and my radio... But on this afternoon, my grandmother opened my door and said, "GarNell, there is a woman out here in the road that says that she is your mother. Now, you can go out there and talk to her if you want to, but she ain't setting foot in this house."

My mother! I was stunned. My mother left me—according to my grandmother—had left me on the porch when I was about two years old and after my father's murder. She had caught the bus to Knoxville where she intended to enroll in business school. She would get a job and then she would come back and get me and we would go to live in Knoxville... But she never came back... Until now.

I went like a sleepwalker and stood on the porch and looked at this woman who stood in the hot sun, staring at the Balsam Mountains. I finally went to stand in front of her, and she was beautiful, just like she looked in the old photographs in my grandmother's little album, and she placed a hand on my head and it was like an electric shock... for I had never been touched like that, and she stroked my cheek... and then she said, "Let's walk."

And we did, down the little dirt trail to the Cope Creek bridge, and then we turned down the little trail that is now Caldwell Street under the big willow trees that used to be there and past the old woman's house where a flock of guineas chattered hysterically as we passed and all the way she asked questions about my life and school and what I did, and what books I read. Then we turned up the little trail that curved and wound through Rhodes Cove, but eventually joined the little trail that ran by my grandparents' house and so we had made a big loop and when we were once more in front of the house where my grandmother sat on the porch, my mother said, "Let's keep walking."

So we did, for several hours, and now my mother was telling me a story that was quite different from the one I had been told and it was all about her life in a little town in Tennessee called Columbia and she was married and she had another son who was named Skip.

"I had to go, Gary Neil," she said, and she said my name distinctly and correctly, not "GarNell" that my grandparents called me. My mother told me a grim story about what her life was like before she married my father, and she told me that her own mother, my other grandmother, was mentally ill and suffered from abscessed teeth that made her scream in pain and that she sometimes attacked her own children. And then my beautiful mother sat down on the bank below Painter's pasture, and she showed me a hole in her leg just behind her knee, and it was deep and ugly and it was where her mother burned her with a poker that she took from the fireplace. She told me her brothers had all run away from home, and the oldest, Arie, had sent her a postcard from Florida, telling her, "Get out, Irene, before Momma kills you." Yes, my mother's name was Irene, and she told me how she had wanted to paint and write, but had never had the opportunity, but perhaps I could do all the things she had wanted to do.

My mother's visit turned into a three-day affair and she came each morning and stood in the road, waiting for me to join her and we continued to walk and talk and plan, and I began to believe that it was all possible. I wanted to believe it would, and when my mother returned to Columbia, Tennessee, we made plans for me to come there, and I indeed did go on an all-day bus journey, but my stay of a week turned into a single day and night and it became obvious that I was an unwanted visitor. My mother's husband refused to talk to me and Skip hated me on sight and sat in his mother's lap and wept, so my mother put me on the bus home to Sylva and we wrote each other, but it was an impossible dream.

In time, my grandmother . . . the one I grew up calling Momma, she relented and told me other brutal facts that made this tragic event even worse . . . When my father was "courting" my mother, her mother refused to let my father visit her and finally, when my father came to see my mother and was turned away, my mother found her father's pistol and shot herself. My grandmother said that when my father and mother were married, my mother's arm was still in a sling. Then my father was murdered by an old drunk, who shot him in the little gas station my father operated. And when I thought the terrible events were over, a relative told me what no one would tell me. That my mother undertook to run the little gas station after my father's death and did so, walking home each night to my grandparents' house . . . until she was attacked and raped one night.

And so finally this impossible story wound to a close. I visited her shortly before her death and she was living in a tiny room with a black-and-white TV and when it came time for me to leave, she handed me a little locket which contained a photograph of her and my father, and she said, "Gary Neil, that is all that is left."

This story is so bleak and grim, it is almost comical. How could one human being experience so much tragedy and still struggle to hope for resolutions and happiness. But, so it is. I am not in the business of creating martyrs, but my little mother was a martyr. I will forever remember her standing there in the road, patiently waiting for me. The last time I talked to her, she was in good spirits. She smiled and took her finger and tapped my head and said, "Gary Neil, what is going to become of all the wonders that are in there?" Well, Momma, it is late in the day, but I will attempt to do something with my life that would please you.

And so I have.

Memory

Well, kind hearts, other than the fact that I love movies and books, I find very little in the current world that I value, and I have developed a distaste for concrete, streetlights, and technology. I yearn to be back on the porch with my grandparents where the nights are unpolluted with sirens and traffic. But I am not foolish about it. I know "the old order changeth, yielding place to new / . . . Lest one good custom should corrupt the world." I hope to impart some reason for valuing our culture, for it was a good one, and if someone doesn't speak up there are some folks that will speak ill of us, of our beliefs and our customs. Don't you believe it. We were a rich and varied culture, full of admirable traits and beliefs, and our current generation should be proud of their roots, their history, and their music. I would like to think that most of what we call Appalachian customs and traditions will live on in this and future generations.

Like most of my peers, I'm slowing down. I feel like a wind-up toy that is running down, and I've lost the key. I have to stop for a little breather on my way to the mailbox; carrying the groceries in from the car has turned into an afternoon (and sometimes, a two-day) project. Getting in and out of my car requires patience and a certain amount of skill. I guess it is natural that I have started looking for alternatives: ways to travel while sitting still. There is TV, of course, but I doze off a lot lately. However, there is another possibility. I've always been blessed (or cursed) with a good memory.

As I sit on my porch in the evening and watch the twilight fade in the Balsams, I've developed a foolish but entertaining habit. For a few moments before darkness comes, I travel. I go to the Pinnacle Knob where I stand for a moment on a rocky crag, feeling a brisk cool breeze on my face as I peer into the distance at Rhodes Cove where an old guy, sitting on his porch, looks back at me. Sometimes, I go to Whiteside Cove and stand in the yard of a cabin called Alexander's Place (it may be gone now), watching trout feed on mayflies in the little creek below the porch.

Time is no barrier either. I can sprint backward to 1953 without even raising a sweat. There I am on the front steps of the Sylva High School with a dozen high school seniors. The boys are all dressed in white, and the girls have on evening dresses. Someone is playing "Dance of the Sugar Plum Fairies," and I am standing next to the athletic (she played basketball) and beautiful Quince Ann Halcombe. With a snap of my fingers, I am parked in front of Troy's Drive-In and Johnny Ray is warbling from the loud speakers on Troy's roof: "If your sweetheart sends a letter of goodbye . . ." Here comes the curb-hop, Kati Lowe, with a tray laden with hotdogs and cokes.

Suddenly, I am sitting in the dark on Mark Watson Field during the Jackson County Centennial. A thunderous version of "The Saber Dance" is playing over the loudspeakers and Bobby Blackwell and I begin to run through the darkness with a bundle of railroad flares. There are two dozen wigwams scattered across the field and each is artfully constructed out of bamboo and tow sacks. We light a flare inside each wigwam which glows with red and orange light as the narrator intones, "The mighty Cherokees lived along the banks of the Tuckasegee," as two-dozen Cherokee maidens (Sylva cheerleaders) dance across the field . . .

Dear Miss Sadie

I doubt that you remember me, but if we could go back almost seventy years to that first time I pushed open the door to that little one-room library on Sylva's main street, and you said, "Now, don't be shy, little boy. Come in, come in!" . . . maybe you would. As I remember, you coaxed me into a room filled with bookcases and a half-dozen stern-looking grown-ups who were reading newspapers. You saw, I think, that I felt that I didn't belong there, so you sat me down at a little table by your desk and asked if I liked dogs and horses.

"Cats, too," I said.

You laughed and said that you couldn't think of any books with cats in them, but you promised to keep an eye out for one. In the meanwhile, you placed a battered copy of *Lassie, Come Home* in my grubby little hands. "Why don't you read a few pages," you said. I did, and suddenly I was in a world that seemed to be created just for me. I checked out the book and took it home to Rhodes Cove, where I lived with my grandparents.

"What are you reading, GarNell?" said Grandpa. I told him about Lassie, and he told me to put the book down, I had chores to do. And so I did, but with every available moment I got, I read about Lassie's long trek home. When I brought the book back, you gave me *My Friend, Flicka*, and after that, *Thunderhead, Son of Flicka* and *Green Grass of Wyoming*. You were always right, because every book you gave me filled me with wonder and hope.

I progressed to *The Black Stallion* and the entire series that followed. Then, one day (I think I was fifteen), you gave me *The Great Gatsby*. For weeks in November I came to sit by the old hissing radiators near your desk and talk about what the green light on the pier signified. Then came *The Red Pony* and *The Yearling*, which I read huddled by the Warm Morning stove in my grandparents' house.

Sometimes, I picked books on my own, and, while you didn't approve of some of them, you let me take home *God's Little Acre* and *I, the Jury*, after giving me a stern look and saying, "If you insist, but you need to get back to books with greatness in them." You were right. Not long after that, you gave me *Look*

Homeward, Angel, and for good or ill, my course was set. I came to realize that I wanted to read books all of my life and I wanted to talk about them. I decided to be a teacher, and, in time, I became a published author and a playwright and storyteller.

Thank you, Miss Sadie. I think of you often and I always see you in that tiny space with a few hundred books that was Sylva's first library. Over the years, you and that little room have become one and the same.

I have been to our new library and it is an awesome, majestic thing. I crept cautiously about marveling at the lofty windows, the polished woodwork, and the furnished offices. I didn't find you, a white-haired lady with a slipping plate that smiled and said to me, "Do you like horses and dogs?"

If they don't have a place for you in that fine, new building, perhaps it is alright if I keep you a place in my memory.

With love,
Gary Carden

Mason Jars in the Flood

When my grandfather built this old farmhouse where I am living now, some eighty years later, he never finished the attic. That was always a dream of his, to finish the attic, and it is now the same unfinished space he dreamed of converting into a bedroom with a feather bed. He had the feather bed, and for years it sat in one corner of the attic, near a window that looked out on the tin roof of the back porch. When we had one of those all-night rains, he would come here in his long johns and he would sink into that feather bed and listen to the soft rain on that tin roof. What did he dream, then? Now that I know a bit about his secret life, perhaps I know what he dreamed about? He had lost his favorite son to a murdering drunk and his dreams of music were gone, but perhaps here, on rainy nights, he revived those dreams.

I remember a night when I followed him up those crooked steps into this unfinished space, filled now with the drone of wasps that fly constantly in the dark, like helicopters surveying some lost battlefield. I *hated* the wasps, and anyone who has been stung by one knows it is a pain that you can't forgive: the sting of a drunken wasp who, as my uncle Albert noted, was "born mad, lived mad, and died mad." But my grandfather always said, "Leave them alone, GarNell."

"Ignore them. If you are going to sleep in this bed, be still!" And so I was, sinking into those ancient feathers and dreaming of cowboys.

BUT THERE WAS A NIGHT I will forever remember, when the soft patter of the rain changed into a drumming, and suddenly it was striking the windows borne by an angry wind, and my grandfather was immediately alert. "Git up, GarNell," he said. "Something is wrong." He rose and crept across the floor, stepping between the stacks of *Grit* magazine and old catalogs. Down the steps, where he found my grandmother already awake to the new threat. She immediately started a fire in the old kitchen stove, for that was her response to all mishaps and dangers. Cook. In moments, I smelled coffee and baking biscuits. My grandfather had his big four-cell flashlight, which he sent into the darkness, where it balked in a few feet, defeated by the heavy downpour.

"Cloudburst," he announced.

That sounded exciting to my ten-year-old brain, and I rushed to the front porch, where I *did* see a strange sight. A creek was finding its way out of the pasture, picking up leaves and dirt in a path that had never known the flow of water. Even as I watched, it was growing in size. In minutes, it was a raging flood. Now, it was laden with tree limbs, walnuts, and—all of a sudden—what appeared to be Jerry Bryson's rabbit trap. Suddenly, I saw what my role was in this growing catastrophe. I would announce and describe the disaster.

I watched the rabbit box, closely followed by a drowned chicken as they came rushing through our yard and disappeared into the cornfield. We had a small branch that ran through the front yard, and now the flood followed it. It moments it passed from a small creek to a raging flood of muddy water and debris.

"Jerry Bryson's rabbit box!" I shouted into the house.

"Dead chicken!" I said.

"Outhouse! Outhouse!" I shouted. "A whole lot of stove wood! Somebody's garden! Corn! Beans! Two rakes and a hoe! Bunch of laundry, shirts and pants and some underwear!!!"

My grandmother came to the door and said, "GarNell, jest hush. You are starting to act like your mother's people." She had that tired and put-upon voice she always got when she talked about my mother's relatives.

"Yes, Momma."

"People can hear you all over this cove like some crazy person shouting about death and destruction. It's bad blood, GarNell. That is what it is." She went back to the kitchen. I got quiet and watched a lot of lumber and most of a barn pass in a mad rush, passing through our cornfield and taking a lot of corn with it.

Suddenly my grandfather announced, "Agnes, I am worried about the cow."

I had been hearing our cow for some time, a doleful bawl that came from our barn. There was a lot of water over there and the cow sounded frightened since she was probably knee-deep in water.

"We need to get her to higher ground, maybe behind the barn. I'll need help."

"I'll go," I said. Grandpa looked at me for a moment, then he shook his head.

"No, me and Agnes can handle it." Off they went, wading through a few feet of water and soon, the sound of the cow bawling stopped. I sat on the porch and watched a lot of muddy water rush through our yard.

THAT WAS WHEN I THOUGHT OF IT. I had not had any playmates in months. Sometimes, people moved into the Cove with kids my age, but they didn't stay long. After a few months, they were gone to Gastonia or High Point, looking for work. Maybe this flood would help me find a playmate.

I went into my grandmother's canning room and began to carry her canning jars to the front porch. After I had most of them lined up, I got my Blue Horse notebook and began to write notes: "Hello! My name is Gary Neil. I live in Rhodes Cove. I drink RC Colas and listen to the *Squeakin' Door*. I read funny books and I have *Batman*, *Red Rider*, *Sub-mariner*, *Superman*, and *Wonder Woman*. Come and play with me." Then I rolled each note up, put it in a Mason jar and screwed the lid on with the rubber seal, and I threw each jar into the flood and watched them go bounding and jumping through the cornfield. I watched them vanish.

That night, I asked Uncle Albert where our branch went. He told me that it went to the Tuckasegee River and after that, it probably made it to the Mississippi and the Pacific Ocean.

"Damn! Then what?"

Albert smiled and said, "Maybe Alpha Centauri."

Each day, I sat on the porch and stared down through our drowned cornfield. Sooner or later, maybe somebody is going to come up that trail with one of my jars.

My grandmother said, "What are you staring down that flooded cornfield for? Looking for my jars? I would like to have my jars back."

Then I dreamed that Debra Paget came up the trail. She looked just like she did in *Broken Arrow* and she had one of my jars. She said, "Okay, Gary Neil. Let's play."

The Raindrop Waltz

My father was a mountain musician—one of those multi-talented fellows who could play anything: banjo, guitar, fiddle, mandolin, piano. Not only that, he also "made up" songs. According to my grandmother, some of them were beautiful and heartbreaking. She once told me that my father would sit on the porch in the dark on warm summer nights and play songs which she said "never had been writ down," and sometimes she would say, "Oh, that was pretty John Lyndon! Play it again." She said that sometimes he would try but would usually quit, saying, "I'm sorry, Momma. It's gone." When I used to sit on the porch with my grandmother, she would tell me a story like that and then smile and say, "Now, ain't that wondrous strange!"

While he was still a teenager, my father was in a string band called the Smoky Mountain String Band that became popular in the region. They played in courthouses, high school gymnasiums, and auditoriums throughout western North Carolina. They became a feature on a radio station in Asheville and began to travel outside the region: Walhalla, South Carolina; Gatlinburg, Tennessee . . . even Nashville a time or two. Mostly though, they performed in a fifty-mile radius of Sylva: Bryson City, Franklin, Webster, Waynesville.

Early on, my father developed a reputation for playing a sentimental piece called "The Raindrop Waltz." Allegedly, it had been written by an unknown, drunken guitar player in an Asheville jail. It was a rainy weekend and the sober musician spent a couple of days staring out of a window in his cell, listening to the rain drip off the roof into a clutter of cans, jars, and bottles. At some point, this fellow thought he recognized a three-quarter-time melody—a waltz—and he picked up his guitar and began to play the melody. After the song became popular, someone wrote a set of lyrics, the kind that yearns for a lost love.

MY FATHER'S GOOD HUMOR earned him the nickname "Happy," and for several years he operated a little gas station called Hap's Place up in the section called Moody's Bottom. This was during the Depression, and the station was usually packed with local musicians and what my grandmother called "trifling loafers." Happy didn't sell much gasoline, but his place became popular for the music. People would even bring chairs and sit on the hill behind the station.

Over the years, I have met several people who remembered my father and actually remembered hearing him play "The Raindrop Waltz." One of them had even been in the string band and told me that my father always played his signature song at the very end, to close out a show. Since it was the Depression and hard times, audiences were hungry for entertainment—so much so that they would object when the band tried to pack up and leave. According to this guy, the audience would get "contrary" and demand that the band keep playing. That was when my father would play "The Raindrop Waltz." Apparently the song became a sort of palliative, and the rambunctious members of the audience would settle down. My mother would tell me the same thing some fifty years later. She said that the song seemed to make everyone docile and content.

The man who killed my father was a local drunk, a little man with big glasses who sat outside the entrance of Hap's Place for several years. He drank wood alcohol, which has killed a lot of alcoholics. The day he shot my father, he showed up with an old, rusty pistol, which he showed to everyone who came to the store. At some point when the store was crowded, the little man with the pistol entered the store and shot my father in the top of the head. He then dropped the gun and ran out of the store and across the railroad tracks to the river, where he sat down on the bank and took his shoes off. Then he waded up the river carrying his shoes. He hid out in the Balsam Mountains, but after several days, he was captured. He never said why he did it. The band attended my father's funeral and played "The Raindrop Waltz" at my grandfather's request.

My father's death wrecked our family. My grandfather never quit grieving the death of a son he considered gifted. In time, he came to feel that music killed my father. My grandmother said that he announced to everyone, "There will be no more music in this house." He took my father's instruments to the attic where they hung alongside each other in that gloomy space—the guitar, the banjo, and the mandolin—like lynched co-conspirators.

A PICTURE WAS MADE OF ME at my father's grave a few weeks after his death. I think I was eighteen months old. My mother once told me that I didn't understand death and sat on the porch each afternoon, waiting for my father to come home. I probably still don't understand Death.

The Drowned Babe

When I was a wee lad, I used to sit on the porch at night with my grandparents and listen to the night sounds on Painter Knob—rain crows, hoot owls, and a wind that moaned like the one that Hank Williams sings about. If it were the fall of the year, my grandmother might be shelling peas and stringing beans that she dropped in a tin pot in her lap. My grandfather was probably sharpening mowing blades with a whetstone and all of this blended together into a kind of plaintive night symphony.

I remember a night when my grandmother stopped snapping and stringing, and after a moment spoke. "There was a baby drowned out there, you know."

Well, no, I didn't know, so I said, "Where?"

"In the spring," she said, pointing to the little springhouse in the front yard. "Wasn't a shelter over the spring then. We kept the milk and butter in a trough on the back porch, and it would be a few years before your granddaddy would build that springhouse. Back then it was just a big, deep pool that bubbled up out of the ground. The people who lived on the ridge told us that spring was hainted." Then, my grandmother went back to her stringing and snapping.

Finally, I said, "Well, did somebody's baby fall in the spring?"

My grandmother smiled in the pale moonlight. "No, GarNell, that baby's mother held her under the water 'til she drowned."

I struggled a bit with that image: a baby drowning in a spring, the hands holding it on the bottom, the baby struggling. "How come that happened?"

"Nobody really knows, but I heard that her people lived at the head of the holler 'n hardly ever come out. She got pregnant and nobody knew who the father was. Her family was ashamed and put her out. She had no place to go and every time she went home, they refused to let her in the house. She got desperate, I reckon, 'n she decided to kill herself 'n the baby."

I was probably nine or ten and all of this upset me. "That's awful!" My granny nodded and went back to the beans and peas. Finally I said, "But she wasn't in the spring with the baby."

Granny stopped again. "No, it wasn't deep enough, I guess. She walked down to the place where Cope Creek meets Scott's Creek and jumped in. They found her later." Granny went back to the beans and peas and I sat for a good while staring at the springhouse.

Finally, I said, "What did you mean about the baby crying?"

Granny settled back in her rocking chair and rocked a bit. Then she said, "Sometimes, that baby cries and the sound seems to come from that spring. It usually happened in the fall and folks used to come from all over to hear it. Upset your granddaddy a bit when folks started coming here in the evening. They would bring blankets 'n they would sit up in the woods. Lots of courting couples came, and sometimes a preacher would preach to them about the lesson to be learned. There were some fools, too. I remember one man that came with a fishing rod and he had a handkerchief tied on the end of the line and he would put the handkerchief in the spring. . . . He would wait until it got dark and he would jerk that handkerchief up 'n the women would scream. Your granddaddy complained to the sheriff and he finally put a stop to it, but it was a while before the people stopped coming."

"Did you ever hear the baby cry?" I asked.

Granny was quiet for a while, but finally, she said, "Just once. Atter that, I stayed in the house. It were a quare sound 'n it seemed to have all the pain in the world in it. It were a sound that contained sadness, loss, and betrayal . . . all wrapped in one cry."

"Well, I don't believe it," I said with the experience and insight of a nine-year-old. "There ain't no such thing as dead babies that cry."

"You are probably right," said Granny. "Just foolishness. Now, I got to go find my flannel sheets. It is going to be cold tonight."

She left me sitting there in the dark, and after Grandpa got up and went inside to build a fire in the fireplace, I sat, watching the fog come down. It crept across the yard and erased the springhouse and the big oak in the front yard, and then there was just me and the night sounds and the fog. Then, I heard it. It was a long, quavering cry, and—like Granny said—it had all of the sadness in the world in it. I fled. I closed the front door and locked it.

When I got in the house, I couldn't find Granny, and Grandpa was already in the bed. I found my way to the kitchen and finally saw her on the back porch. "Where have you been?" I said.

She said she was checking on the chicken house because she heard something prowling around. Then, she smiled and said, "Why? What is wrong?"

I finally said, "That was you, wasn't it?"

She shook her head. "Sometimes, I worry about you. What was me? You are a quare young'en."

THE DROWNED BABE

WHEN I WENT TO COLLEGE and got interested in folklore, I read a book about Ireland that said that rural Ireland was full of haunted springs and that there was a story about a drowned baby in every one of them. Now, I am living in my grandparents' old home, and when I sit on the porch at night, I am aware of where our springhouse once stood. Swept away now, like the night sounds that have retreated to give room for car horns and sirens. Are they gone, then, or are they there beneath the noise: the night sounds . . . and the cry of a baby?

Jack Frost

When I was nine years old and in the fourth grade at Sylva Elementary School, I found myself sitting next to Betty Tuttle, the daughter of the minister at First Methodist Church. Betty had pigtails and dimples and a way of batting her eyes that totally unhinged me. I was smitten and followed Betty everywhere. She didn't seem to mind. I followed her home each afternoon and sat on her front porch telling her all about my heroes, Lash LaRue, Johnnie Mack Brown, Durango Kid, and Gene Autry. For a while, she attended Saturday "westerns" with me at the Ritz. We ate popcorn, drank Pepsis and cheered for Lash, Johnnie, Durango, and Gene. When I think of Betty now, I always remember the smell of Milk Duds and Cracker Jack.

Eventually, Betty invited me to attend the Methodist Youth Fellowship and, since Betty herself would be there, I joined immediately. The Christmas season was approaching, and I learned that the MYF had planned a big pageant with music and costumes. One of the Sunday school teachers announced that she intended to cast a play called *Naughty Jack Frost* and that everyone would have a part. Within a few moments, the teacher had cast over thirty characters—mostly elves and fairies—and everyone was singing and dancing. Except me.

Then, the teacher announced that the lead character in the play was Jack Frost. She said that she needed a nine-year-old boy who was "uninhibited" and would be willing to run, jump, and "laugh like a little demon." When she asked the group who should be Jack Frost, Betty Tuttle said, "That sounds like Gary."

So, against all odds, a runty little fellow who lived in Rhodes Cove with his grandparents became Jack Frost in the Christmas Pageant at the town church. Within a week, my grandmother had made me a costume out of one of my uncle Albert's navy uniforms. Bell-bottomed pants and a bib shirt, altered and scaled down to fit my scrawny frame. I was covered with cotton balls, cranberries and holly leaves. For two weeks, I attended rehearsals each evening where I learned to "freeze" all those elves and fairies.

This is how it worked. Each time that the elves and fairies danced and sang, Jack Frost would dash into their midst with an evil laugh. He would then pause and when he had everyone's attention he would reveal his "freezing finger," which was a long, white, boney thing that encased Jack's forefinger. Jack would then wiggle his eyebrows, pause dramatically, flourish his terrible digit, and then freeze a cute little female elf or fairy.

"EEEEEEEK!" would squeak the elves, Edith, Leah, and Joyce, who would then cringe, whimper, and dash offstage.

"HAA, HAA, HAA!" said Jack, who would then dash away to freeze other hapless sprites named Doris, Jean, and Polly.

This sequence would continue until the stage was bare except for Jack. Finally, some fairy queen (looking like the Good Witch in the Land of Oz) would arrive and scold Jack Frost. "Naughty, naughty Jack," she said, and then she cast a magic spell that caused Jack's long, icy finger to disappear. The Good Fairy then urged Jack to change his ways and become one of her happy sprites. Then the fairies and elves rushed back on stage and hugged the defrosted Jack and the entire group sang Christmas carols together.

TO BE PERFECTLY HONEST, I was not happy with the play's conclusion. I had found something wonderfully fulfilling in the act of freezing the girls and sending them scurrying offstage. For weeks after the pageant, I pondered the discovery that I liked being the center of attention. Then, one day at recess, I found myself sitting in the great jack pine thicket with my classmates. This was the place where we ate our lunch each day, sometimes trading with each other—a banana for a peanut butter and jelly sandwich, or a Little Debbie for a dozen vanilla wafers. Betty Tuttle was there with a Pepsi and a half-dozen deviled egg halves.

"Hi, Jack," she said. The entire group turned to look at me.

"Where is your finger?" said Edith, Leah, and Joyce.

"Gone," I said.

"Where is your nifty white costume?" said Doris, Jean, and Polly.

"Gone, too," I said.

I noticed that my friends had lost interest in me, as I reached in my own little brown poke and pulled out a tomato sandwich, some of grandmother's teacakes, and a Pepsi.

"That's okay!" said Betty. "Tell us about Lash, Johnny, Durango, and Gene!"

I suddenly found that I had an alternate to that icy digit. Again, I sprang into their midst like Jack Frost, but I knelt and said, "Okay, I'm going to tell you how Lash LaRue saved poor Widow Barlow's ranch and ran the evil banker, Vernon Skaggs, out of town . . ."

And so it began. I learned to tell stories to my classmates, acting out all of the exciting parts . . . like when Lash was ambushed by some gunfighter hid in the jack pines, or when he stood off an Indian raid with nothing but his whip. When my classmates cheered, I knew that I had found my place. Over the years, the tales got longer and more elaborate.

SEVERAL YEARS AGO, I met Betty Tuttle in Boone, where I was attending a storytelling festival. We talked about Sylva and the

Methodist Youth Fellowship and Jack Frost. I told her that I owed her a debt . . . Betty *and* Jack Frost. I think my storytelling started with that Christmas program.

"Maybe freezing pixies and fairies was a beginning," she said, "but you were already fated to make a living by telling lies and tall tales."

Yeah, well, thank you, Betty . . .

I guess.

Uncle Albert

Kind hearts, I have been thinking about my uncle Albert, the only uncle that was kind to me . . . the uncle that my grandmother called Babe because he was the youngest . . . the one that slept in the back bedroom and washed dishes in Velt's Café for a while and came home late at night with an armful of "funny books" and magazines with titles like *Amazing Tales* and *Other World* and read them until he finally went to sleep, usually around three o'clock, and in the morning I would crawl into his bedroom where his clothes were scattered everywhere and the dresser was covered with the stuff he carried in his pockets . . . change and a rabbit's foot and a Trojan protective rubber that was several years old and worn to an ancient look, one that he carried each night "just in case." But of course I was only interested in the comic books that were beneath the bed—beneath Albert's face with his snoring mouth open—and I would gather this treasure and crawl back through the kitchen, clutching *Batman* and *Sub-mariner* and *Captain Marvel*, back to my bed on the old wicker couch in the living room, and there I would proceed to "destroy my young mind" with the amazing and magical adventures of my heroes.

I loved my uncle Albert because he not only shared his comic books but also encouraged me to read them and often talked to me as he drank coffee at the kitchen table, talked to me about Krypton and what SHAZAM meant. He probably did me a lot of harm, because he loved to tell me fantastic lies . . . lies that I believed. I remember that he used to give me a ride to town on Saturday to see the western at the Ritz, and I remember that there used to be a large number of tombstones on the hill next to the Ritz, and one Saturday when we got to town before the Ritz opened, Uncle Albert parked across the street and pointed to all of those tombstones and asked me if I knew why they were there, and of course, I didn't. Albert said, "Kid, those are the graves of the bad men that get killed at the Ritz every Saturday," and I gawked and said, "Ahhhhhh, no," and he said yes and he told me a marvelous lie about how men who were condemned in prisons in the South—condemned to be executed—were given a choice: Did they want to die in the electric chair, or did they want to go to Sylva and end up in a shootout with Gene Autry or Hopalong, or Durango Kid? There was a slight chance that they might survive the gunfight at the Ritz, and if they did, they were given a bus ticket to Atlanta and a second chance at life. I stared at my Uncle Albert and said, "Ahhhhh, no." He said yes and I believed it and I told it to my best friend, Charlie Kilpatrick, and he believed it too. We even planned to sneak backstage behind the screen at the Ritz to see if we could find the dead outlaws, but Mr. Moody caught us . . . and that is another story.

Charlie's Funny Books

That cold wind that has been woofing in the eaves the last few weeks reminds me of my childhood in the Sylva Elementary School. SES was a two-story brick building on what is now Mark Watson Field, and it had been officially condemned several times before I graduated and went on to high school in the late 1940s. On windy days in March, we could feel the school literally move.

Somewhere in the bowels of that building, great metal girders shifted. I would look across the aisle at Charlie K., a little chubby kid who always wore peppermint-striped T-shirts, and he would make his eyes get big and round and he would whisper, "It's coming down!" Then he would imitate the sound the building made: "EEEEERRRRKKKK! Hear that? You feel the floor moving?"

Charlie K. was my best friend. We ended up together because, as our teachers said, we shared "an imaginative proclivity." Charlie K. and I knew that this was teachers' talk for saying we were weird in the same way. Like me, Charlie K. loved funny books, Saturday westerns and "Owl Shows" (which is what they called the scary movies at the Ritz Theater on Saturday night). By the time we were in the third grade, Charlie had shown me his secret hideouts. He had two. One was under the Sylva Elementary School and the other was the inside of Sylva's abandoned movie theater, the Lyric.

Beneath the flooring of the school, Charlie had found a dark hole where we could sit and listen to the building creak while we ate our bag lunches. Charlie said that the shadowy recesses beneath the school were where Dracula and Frankenstein's monster stayed between appearances at the Owl Show. Charlie had a talent for making me see the same thing he saw. "Don't you see him, Gary Neil? Behind that big brick pillar? There! I can see his teeth!" Eventually, I would see Bela's fangs or the knobs on Boris's head, and as the dark figures lurched slowly toward us, Charlie and I would flee. Leaving our lunch, we would emerge with thundering hearts into the bright sunlight where we would describe our narrow escape to our classmates, who would look knowingly at each other and smile.

However, in terms of atmosphere, the Lyric Theater far surpassed Sylva Elementary. Every window was boarded up and every door was locked and wrapped in chains—but Charlie K. knew how to get inside. After crawling through a network of vents and old storage rooms, we would emerge in the murky interior, where rotting curtains stirred in the damp air and little shafts of light struggled to reach the rotting stage and moldy seats. I remember that there was always the sound of dripping water and that families of squeaking rats would skitter up the dark aisles. Eventually, Charlie would point to the great sagging balcony that seemed to float in the darkness. "There he goes! See him, Gary Neil? The Wolf Man! He's coming for us!" And he was, because I saw him too! Lon Chaney Jr. dropped from the balcony and growled and Charlie K. and I were gone, back through the tunnels and vents . . . back into the sunshine and the safety of the ordinary world.

But the biggest treat was yet to come—Charlie K.'s funny books. We would climb College Hill, stopping at our favorite foxholes to fight valiantly with the "sons of Nippon" who infested the kudzu thickets along the way. When we finally reached Charlie's house, we would tiptoe through the kitchen into a screened-in porch where a huge chest-of-drawers sat against the wall. Each drawer was labeled with names like CAPTAIN MARVEL, THE HUMAN TORCH, NYOKA, and THE PHANTOM. Inside, the comics were chronologically arranged in neat stacks. Charlie K. had everything!

Thanks to Charlie's collection, I learned the origin of all of my favorite heroes and could follow their careers from their birth to the present. For example, I knew that "The Heap," who was a kind of walking brush pile, had once been a famous German fighter pilot before he crashed into a swamp and emerged as some kind of human-plant hybrid that wandered the world destroying evil humans. Heaven help you if the Heap grabbed you in his twiggy embrace. We knew that Billy Batson (Captain Marvel) had a long-lost twin sister who became her brother's equal by saying the magic word, "SHAZAM." She looked a little like a high school cheerleader, but she could fly.

Usually, Charlie K.'s mother would put an end to our comic book session by staring at the two of us until I got uncomfortable. "You need to go home, Gary Neil. It is almost dark and your grandmother will be worried." In those long, summer evenings with Charlie K.'s funny books, I noticed that his mother looked at his wonderful collection with distaste. "Reading those things will rot your brain," she would say. "Them silly books are going to make idiots of the two of you." She always ended this little tirade with a threat: "One of these days while you are at school, I'm going to burn them! I'll make a huge pile in the back yard, pour a quart of coal oil on them and strike a match!"

I remember one afternoon when Charlie K.'s mother had made her threat and returned to the kitchen. Charlie K. watched her go and then said, "That's not my mother, you know." I laid down *Sheena, Queen of the Jungle*, and forgot about the terrible revenge that she was about to bring to Ungawa, the witch doctor.

"What?!"

Charlie K. laid down his *Captain America*, leaned forward and whispered, "Neither one of these people that I live with are related to me!"

Then he told me a marvelous tale. Charlie K. said that his real parents were wealthy English aristocrats who had devoted their lives to fighting the Nazis. They built an underground lab in Africa where they designed atomic weapons. When the evil "Axis powers" learned their location, Hitler sent an assassination squad to Africa. In a hushed whisper, Charlie K. told me that his parents were killed, but that he was smuggled to America, where his father's friends arranged for him to be reared in secret. When he reaches the "age of consent," his father's atomic squadron will come to Sylva and spirit him away in a black helicopter. Charlie K. will then take command of his father's loyal forces, who will launch a coup to avenge the murder of his parents. Wow!

SIXTY YEARS HAVE PASSED since Charlie swore me to secrecy. I guess it is safe to talk about it now. I like to think that he is happy and well in Africa. I wonder if he needs an assistant.

Bad Blood

Kind hearts, I dreamed last night—or maybe I just remembered—about an old doll that I had when I was around four years old. It was as big as me, and I remember that its head was mostly gone, since I dragged it by the foot every place I went. Up and down the steps to the attic, up and down the big concrete and rock steps in front of the house, through the cornfield, to the barn . . . every place that I went, I dragged that poor doll. It was an old-fashioned doll and had once had a dress, but I remember that its stuffings were coming out. At some point, my grandfather took the doll away and I spent hours looking for it, but my grandfather had banished my brainless doll to some unknown land where it sat on a shelf with all of the injured toys, like the little toy soldier in the poem. So, I lost my sole playmate, who had been perfect since it was totally submissive and never complained as it went clunk, clunk, clunk behind me.

My grandfather saw my behavior as yet another indication that I had "bad blood," and he talked to me often about what that meant. In the world today, "bad blood" means that there is a lot of anger between two individuals or families or nations, but in 1940 in Rhodes Cove, "bad blood" meant that you had been doomed—damned!—by your genes. As far as I can tell, nothing has changed. People still believe that you can be destined to be poor, stupid, mean, and/or helpless by your ancestors.

My grandparents were typical of the traditional Appalachia family that inherited a host of bad traits from their ancestors. If someone came by with a tragic bit of news about a local alcoholic or a family that were starving and poorly clothed, my grandmother would shake her head and say, "Well, they can't help it, they have bad blood." And then she would go on to cite proof by recounting the shortcomings of their ancestors, going back for several generations. "Pitiful," she would say, "but they can't help it." She would go on to describe the many hopeless attempts to help them in the past. Ah, but no, she would insist, "They are doomed." After that, she would repeat her favorite judgment: "There ain't nothing you can do about it."

WHEN I GOT POLIO, I guess I was eight or ten. I survived, although I remember long whispered conversations about my condition and—given my puny health—my demise. But, against all odds, I lived: scrawny, awkward, and my spine was messed up, but unlike some of my playmates who survived with withered legs or arms, I returned to school . . . and there was Charlie F., who was on crutches now and had a withered leg, and I talked to him at school and told my grandmother about him. "Poor boy," she proclaimed. "He has bad blood." And then she and my grandfather discussed the possibility that I also had it—"from his mother's side," which had a generous supply of drunks, the mentally challenged, and folks with violent tempers. I was cautioned by my grandfather, "Fight it, boy. Fight it! You might have enough Carden in you to overcome it." Those lectures frightened me, and I imagined this dark flood of bad blood rushing through me.

As time went on, I was told a series of tales about my "bad blood" relatives, and I often felt that my grandparents were watching me, believing that they would see the first indication that I was doomed, and they were alarmed when I read funny books and talked to imaginary playmates. On we went.

A doctor gave me a back brace, but I wore it one day and took a bit of kidding at recess, so after that I walked up in the pasture each morning and took the back brace off and hung it on a limb, returning each evening to put it on again before entering the house. With a bit of luck, I made it through high school and got a Vocational Rehab scholarship to go to Western Carolina Teacher's College . . . They later revoked it because I took a major in theater and someone at VR told me that I was "dabbling in the effeminate arts instead of practical courses." So my grandfather paid for my last year in college.

I graduated along with Charlie F. who was on crutches, and I got a job teaching in Waynesville and so did Charlie F. and when I told my grandmother that Charlie F. was going to ride with me to Waynesville each morning, she said, "Poor boy! Bad blood . . . doomed to be worthless." And on we went. At the end of the year, the superintendent of schools in Haywood got Charlie F. a scholarship to get his doctorate. Charlie did and went on to become department head at a major college. I told my grandmother about his success and I had to repeat it several times. She was astonished.

She said, "Don't they know who he is?!"

AND SO, LIFE GOES ON. Charlie F. died recently, and his obituary was a lengthy record of success and achievement, despite his "bad blood."

Abner, the Wild Monkey of the Smokies

I don't remember the origin of this story . . . I have told it many times over the years, but it always changes when I do, taking abrupt turns onto side roads . . . and suddenly I am lost in Little Canada, or maybe Cades Cove . . . and I am almost out of gas. Scary, but then up ahead, there are bright lights and it looks like another country . . . My God, it is the Cherokee Indian Fair! I vaguely remember hearing a story some seventy years ago about a monkey that unintentionally killed himself with his owner's straight razor . . . and then I resurrected him when I heard Carl Lambert tell me about the monkey that he took home from the Cherokee Indian Fair, wrapped in a burlap sack, and suddenly it is a cold October night full of bells, whistles, and laughter, strange smells: cotton candy and charred meat. The monkey has diarrhea and shivers in his foul sack in a dark cage and an old man named Carl is prodding him with a stick.

"Still alive," says the old man.

"Yeah, well, so?" says the man in the bowler hat.

"Give you ten dollars."

Bowler Hat snorts, then says, "Okay. But to be honest, I don't think he is going to live another day."

The old man lifts the monkey from the sack and stares at the little wizened face. "I am goin' to call him Abner."

"You want a clean sack?"

"No, I'll just drop him in here." The monkey settles inside the old man's bib overalls that smell of tobacco and beef jerky.

"Suit yourself," says Bowler Hat and snatches the bill from the old man's fingers with practiced ease.

SO ABNER CAME TO LIVE with the old man in an old farmhouse in Big Cove on the Cherokee lands. Carl fed him cornbread and buttermilk and souse meat and the monkey thrived. Before long, he was swinging in the rafters and peering through the windows at a strange world. Chickens and hounds. A cow and a mule.

Although Abner came when he was called, he was "a free agent." That meant that he did what he wanted. When he ventured outside and explored the barn, he frightened the chickens. Abner got a perverse pleasure out of reducing the chicken house to pandemonium when he swung through the rafters, leaving a storm of feathers and dust. In time, he learned to ride the hound and spent exciting nights riding the poor creature through the moonlit forest. He left in his wake a kind of tidal wave of cackles, screams, hoots, and trills, as the creatures of the woods took note of his passage.

Abner still came when he was called, but his absences from Carl's kitchen became longer and longer. A few days and then an entire week. Carl's neighbors kept him informed about the disturbances: tales of Abner pursuing foxes on the backs of blue tick hounds. They said he made the dogs run faster by biting their ears, his legs wrapped around them like a Saturday cowboy. People complained when Abner took to plucking chickens, leaving great clouds of feathers wafting through the woods. Dogs' owners threatened to shoot him.

A kind of legend developed about Abner, the Wild Monkey of the Smokies. Carl was a popular storyteller, and on winter nights, he would entertain the neighbors with stories of Abner's adventures. On one of his treks into town, Abner had raided a craft shop and come away with a rebel cap that became a permanent accessory, and many tourists came out of the Smokies with incoherent tales of a monkey with a rebel cap who attacked campgrounds at night, vanishing into the darkness with gaudy clothes, candy, and food.

Ah, but when the heavy snows came and the campgrounds closed, Abner came home. Carl said that it was a kind of hibernation, he guessed. Deprived of excitement, Abner became morose and depressed, spending hours staring out of the window at the snow. Then there came a year when he did not return. For several years, there were stories of a monkey riding the windbuffeted hemlocks and staring down at startled travelers.

NOW, LET'S CHANGE GEARS and let me say that I have always identified with Abner, the Wild Monkey of the Smokies. Hell, I am Abner. From the time he was plucked from that dark cage until he vanished into the dark wood, I felt an empathy with that solitary creature. He lived in a world without companionship (there weren't any other monkeys out there!) and although he made efforts to befriend and live with other creatures (dogs, humans, and chickens), he was (I am) a solitary being. Yeah, I have tried too, but I have so little in common with others, it is a hopeless pursuit. Yes, I'm only fit company for Abner and I think I would enjoy that: Abner and I high in a hemlock riding the wind.

Some have abandoned me so they could devote more time to seeking fame of some sort, or fortune. A few have gone in search of God . . . a search that takes all of their time and energy. Adieu, travelers and pilgrims. Abner and I bid you farewell. You all go on ahead, now. We will catch up.

I HAVE BEEN THINKING that perhaps I could teach Abner to read. It would be quite a challenge ... but then, we have nothing but time. Certainly, there are wonderful possibilities. What would Abner think of Cormac McCarthy? I think he would love A. E. Housman. How about the *Rubaiyat*? Hey, then there is Yeats, a poet after a wild monkey's heart! For, like Abner, I was born into a world where both reading and friendship are becoming a kind of lost art. Perhaps Abner and I could start a secret sect that ... *reads* stuff. Rediscover poetry. Write a play. I heard once that Abner loved Elvis. So okay, maybe I can lure him out. Maybe if I go to Deep Creek tonight and sing "Can't Help Falling in Love," I might tease him out. I do a pretty good Elvis when there is no one around to judge ... Or maybe, if I sing long enough, he will hear the Righteous Brothers.

Lonely rivers flow, to the sea, to the sea, to the open arms of the sea ...

Come out, Abner!

Come to Rhodes Cove and sit with me in the fog and listen to the rain crows on Painter Knob. I think their sad coo will soothe your mad heart! We still have a little while before the streetlights and pavement run us off to some dark holler ... to Black Rock or Linville Gorge.

I'll be coming home, wait for me ...

Come out, you rascal.

Grandfather's New Dodge Pickup

Well, kind hearts, it has come time to talk about 1954, when my grandfather banished me. That is right. He told my grandmother, because he could not bear to talk to me, "Agnes, tell him to go live with Albert in Brevard. I can't stand the sight of him." So it was that I collected my ragged clothes along with my Levis and my few decent shirts and put them in the back seat of Albert's car. I said my goodbyes to my friends down at the pool hall, and the next day I was sleeping on a couch in Albert's house, where I watched the *Mickey Mouse Club* each afternoon when I got home from my new job at the Silverstein Tannery.

It was a bleak and hopeless time. I was working in the green hide room and eating dinner each day in the wretched Green Fly Café, also owned by the tannery. There were days when I called my grandmother (whom I called Momma) on Albert's telephone and asked if I could come home.

"Not yet, GarNell. Yore Granddaddy is still awful mad."

What did I do that got me sent to a hell of rotting hides and a stench that lingered in my clothes for days? Well, I am still ashamed, for it was hard to forgive.

MY GRANDFATHER BOUGHT a new Dodge pickup. It was the first new vehicle that he had owned in his life. Prior to this, he had bartered for weeks for a variety of automobiles that were afflicted with faulty parts, and he traded cars as often as he did cows. Ah, but finally here it was, sitting in the driveway and it still had that "new car smell." When I asked to drive it downtown and back, he hesitated, but he finally agreed, and since I was only going to the Ritz to stand for two hours and stare at the girl who took up tickets, my grandfather felt sure that no great harm could come to his new truck.

But none of us reckoned on Jimmy Stovall. As I stood by the popcorn machine staring at Doris, Jimmy showed up. He stood about, occasionally asking me to give him a ride to Cherokee where his latest passion flower lived. When I said I had no intention of going to Cherokee, he said, well how about giving him a ride to the telephone booth where he could call her. No, Jimmy, I am not leaving this theater.

"Well," said Jimmy, "Loan me that new truck long enough to go to the telephone booth." To call his true love.

I did it. I handed him the keys to my grandfather's new truck. "Be back here in twenty minutes," I said. Jimmy saluted me and sped away.

Now, the terrible truth. Jimmy Stovall had no intention of going to a telephone booth. Jimmy Stovall was on his way to Cherokee at a pretty good clip. He wasn't back in twenty minutes. He wasn't back in an hour. And when the Ritz closed and I was left standing outside under the dark marquee, I became nervous. It was then that the local taxi driver, Scrup Lewis, pulled over and said, "Hey, Gary, anybody hurt in that wreck?"

And I said, "What wreck?"

Then Scrup pointed to the Cogdill car lot where a totally destroyed Dodge pickup sat.

I go back inside the Ritz and ask Mr. Moody if I can use his phone to call the Stovalls, and when I did, Mrs. Stovall said that Jimmy was in the hospital with some minor cuts and bruises, but she was glad that I had called. Would I please go look in the wrecked truck and see if I could find Jimmy's glasses? Thank you. And she was gone and I was left with the awesome duty of telling my grandfather what had happened to his truck.

IT GETS WORSE. Mr. Stovall refused to accept any responsibility for what Jimmy had done. So my grandfather had lost his new truck and I was in Brevard sitting each afternoon with the stench of rancid hides on me as I sang with Darlene, "Mickey Mouse! Mickey Mouse!"

The Green Fly Café

Most storytellers will tell you that their best yarns are frequently drawn from their worst experiences in life. I guess that is the blessing of the oral tradition: transmutation. Moments of personal shame, anguish, or suffering undergo a wonderful transition with the passage of time. Like William Wordsworth's comment about how poetry emerges when it is "recollected in tranquility," I have found rich deposits of whimsy and humor in unpleasant events that happened over sixty years ago. For example, take the summer of 1954 when I worked for the Silverstein Tannery in Brevard.

I grew up in a remote cove in Jackson County, raised by my grandparents, an old Scots-Irish couple who observed my peculiarities with anxiety. In addition to an obsession with comic books and cowboy movies, I frequently got in trouble in school, and by the time I reached high school, many teachers had expressed concern about my inability to "tell the difference between fantasy and reality." After I also let my friend wreck his new truck, my grandfather's solution was to send me off to live with my uncle in Brevard for the summer. "Put him to work," said my grandfather. "Maybe a good dose of making-a-living will straighten him out."

So I came to work in the Silverstein Tannery, where my uncle was the bookkeeper, and was given a job in the buffing room, which was next to a huge storage area called "the green hide room." To the great amusement of my fellow workers, I immediately became ill from the tannery's foul smell. Green hides are covered with decaying flesh, which must be stripped away before the hides can be converted into shoe leather. The smell that emanated from that room hung like a dark cloud over the tannery and the surrounding area.

The company-owned café where all of the workers ate was next to the green hide room and was called the Green Fly. After a week, I adjusted to the smell and managed to eat my daily portion of pintos, collard greens, and cornbread with reasonable gusto. Every worker had a tab at the café, and on payday (Saturday morning) his tab was deducted from his earnings. Since the Green Fly also had punchboards and pinball machines, some workers actually ended up owing money to the store after cashing their checks.

The buffing room was located in a large, barn-like structure, and its purpose was to convert inferior hides into acceptable shoe leather. This meant that thin hides that were pocked with holes were "improved," or brought up to minimum standards. Our job was to apply a nauseous, yellow gunk to the hides. This operation had to be repeated many times and was carried out by placing the hides on a table where four workers stood with huge brushes strapped to their forearms and alternately dipped the brushes in the yellow gunk and then spread it, like lemon cake icing, over the hides. After the workers had created a thick layer, the hides were allowed to dry. Then each was placed on the buffing machine, where a great metal cylinder literally beat the gunk into the hide until it was absorbed. After each hide was buffed several times, it acquired an acceptable thickness and could be sold for low-grade shoe leather.

A bucket of water stood by each table, and when the brushes became clogged, we would clean them in the buckets. The water level in the bucket was always about half full because the buffing machine caused the floor to shift like the deck of a ship. The water sloshed back and forth in rhythm to the machine. All of this created a deafening noise and rendered conversation impossible. We all learned to communicate in a kind of buffing-room mime of hand gestures and facial expressions.

Work in the buffing room was mentally numbing, and the workers developed a mindless, repetitive routine which lasted for two-hour intervals. We received two fifteen-minute breaks—one in the morning and one in the afternoon, and they were deducted from our pay. During the break, workers would go to the toilets or walk to the loading docks to smoke or to stare aimlessly about. Many simply sat on the floor next to the workstation. I remember one colorful fellow who climbed on the idle buffing machine during the breaks and preached to his fellow workers, exhorting them to find Jesus.

Other than me, my work station consisted of Lil, a gigantic blonde woman who resembled Boris Karloff, a small man named Westley who constantly hummed and yodeled cowboy songs during our breaks, and a talkative man named Manard who kept up a constant monologue about his exploits: hunting, fights, and epic drunks. During the breaks, Lil lay on the floor, inert as a fallen tree, and slept. Westley did a passing good imitation of his hero, Eddie Arnold, and his all-time favorite, "Cattle Call." When

Westley yodeled, Manard and I fled to the loading dock, where Manard talked about his Saturday nights that he spent driving around Brevard with a bottle of John Paul Jones whiskey and a paper sack full of cherry bombs (bought each Saturday afternoon in South Carolina, where both whiskey and fireworks were available). His greatest joy in life consisted of lighting cherry bombs and pitching them through the window of his car when he was passing a crowd outside a theater or a church.

Sometimes, the monotony of the buffing room routine was broken by a visit from the owner. He wore fancy riding pants, carried a little leather jockey's whip, and was usually accompanied by two white poodles. Sometimes I would look up from spreading gunk on a hide and find him watching me. Usually he would say something like, "Faster, faster," while the dogs barked at us and he popped his whip against his pants leg. Then he would walk away to watch the buffing machine.

I LASTED TWO MONTHS at the Silverstein Tannery. When I received word that my grandfather was willing to let me return home—provided that I met certain conditions—I collected my last check (twelve dollars) and boarded a Trailways bus for Sylva. However, during my last week, Manard took two days of sick leave and then returned with the lower part of his face encased in adhesive tape. It occurred to me that he looked a bit like the Mummy, and I got a kick out of watching him and Lil shuffle about like they were in Dr. Frankenstein's laboratory. Manard had a little slit cut over his mouth so he could insert his beloved Lucky Strikes.

For the first time since I had met Manard, I was genuinely curious about his weekend adventures. When the buffing machine finally shut down for the morning break and Westley began to yodel "Oh-dah-letty-who," I followed Manard to the dock and watched as he carefully poked a cigarette into his slit and lit up. "So, what happened to you?" I said. It was a little hard to understand him since he had lost most of his teeth, but this is the gist of what he said:

"Well . . . Last Saturday after drawin' my pay, I drove down to the South Caroliny line whar I bought a fifth of JPJ and a sack of cherry bums. I come on back to Brevard 'cause I knowed thet there was a big church revival down on Carver Street. I set outside thet church 'til almost midnight, sippin' JPJ and listenin' to WNOX in Knoxville. Drunk thet whole fifth 'n bout the time the church clock started strikin' midnight, them folks come pourin' out of thet church. I rolled a winder down, 'n usin' my cigarette, I lit one of them cherry bums, 'n I throwed my cigarette out the winder 'n put thet cherry bum in my mouth."

RECENTLY I READ in a regional newspaper that a historical society in Brevard intended to publish an oral history of the region's tanneries, and they were soliciting personal reminiscences from former employees. Suddenly, it all came back. The Green Fly Café, the buffing machine, the white poodles, and Lil asleep by her workstation. I'm not sure if "nostalgia" is the appropriate word for my memories, and I have serious doubts about the historical society's wishes to know how I feel about the old Silverstein Tannery, green hides, and the buffing room. However, I will admit that I laugh every time I think of Manard with a cherry bomb in his mouth.

Gall Lake

Back in the 1970s when I worked for the Eastern Band of Cherokee as a grant writer, I met a Cherokee named Johnson Cotoaster who worked with a program that provided transportation to the hospital for the elderly and ill. At the time, I had an office in the Aquoni building, where the program was located, and on days when business was slow or it was raining, I used to talk to Johnson. We liked to sit on the big couch in the lobby and watch it rain, and it was then that Johnson would tell me stories.

One day, he suddenly said, "I saw one of the little people yesterday. I was coming back from Smokemont and there he was, naked as a jaybird and he was trying to get across 441 when a car came out of the Park at a pretty good clip and he just walked backwards into the brush. I thought that was funny, to see him walk backwards."

We watched it rain for a while and then I said, "How tall was he?"

Johnson turned and looked at me and said, "Oh, I didn't see you sitting there, Unegi." ("Unegi" is what Cherokees call white people.) "I know that you don't believe in the little people."

I said, for the sake of conversation, "Let's pretend that I do believe. How tall was he?"

Johnson thought for a moment, and then he said, "He would have come up to my belt buckle. They are mischievous and love to play tricks on Cherokees. Sometimes they throw rocks on my roof late at night."

We watched it rain for a while. It was one of those slow rains that falls in slow sheets and there was nothing to do but watch it clean the dirty pavement. Finally, Johnson said, "My grandfather told me lots of stories about the little people. He also told me about scary creatures like the Uktena and the Dakow and the Taliwah. Maybe I will tell you about them some rainy day. He told me about the Gall Place and then he took me to see it."

There was a long silence then and I knew that Johnson was kidding me. He knew that—sooner or later—I would ask for details. He was right. Finally, I said, "So what is the Gall Place?"

Johnson gave me a cool look. "Don't rush me, Unegi."

"Sorry," I said. I knew better, so I waited for Johnson to continue. He always did.

"My own grandfather told me about the Gall Place. He is gone now. Peace to his ashes, sorrow to his going. My mother did not want him to tell me stories, and she would interrupt him, telling him to not fill my head with foolishness and superstitions. My mother worked as a teacher's aide at the big school and she wanted me to become a teacher and maybe work for the BIA [the Bureau of Indian Affairs]. So my grandfather would wait until she was watching TV and then he would tell me stories about magic and wonder. He had diabetes and he had a hard time breathing, but he could tell stories that left me dreaming about giant fish and great hawks. He said Gall Place is a magic lake that has purple water. Fog and mist cover it and it also has the ability to move. Sometimes it is deep in the Park beyond New Found, and then it will move to Cades Cove or back beyond the Cowee Mountains. Strange birds live at the Gall Place and when you get near, you can hear their cries as they fly through the lake's fog.

"One night when he was very sick, struggling to breathe, he said, 'Johnson, would you like to see the Gall Place?' I got very excited and he had to warn me that my mother could not know about this. He peered into the living room where my mother sat watching one of her movies. She often went to sleep in that flickering blue light. I asked him when we were going.

"'Tomorrow,' he said. 'Can you be up by 5:00?'

"'It will still be dark then,' I said.

"'Yes,' he said. 'We will push my old truck off so your mother will not hear it crank. Be at the truck at 5:00.'

"I was there and we jump-started it, rolling downhill from the house. We drove into the Park and took an old logging road that went for several miles through laurel thickets and ended up in a creek bed.

"'Now we walk,' said my grandfather.

"It was then that I noticed that my grandfather was perspiring heavily and his breathing was becoming labored. The sun was coming up when he came to a ridge top. Beyond, I saw the strange birds that wheeled and dove in and out of the fog.

'We are here,' said Grandfather. 'I was afraid I would not make it.'

"So I saw the Gall Place. As I watched, hundreds of animals came out of the forest and waded into the lake. Old bears with gray hair, wounded deer, many with arrows in their bodies, great elk limped into the lake and yes, I saw Cherokees who were ill, women and children wading into the water. I understood that the waters healed them and when they climbed out of the lake on the distant shore, they were young again. Vibrant and alive. There was a great forest beyond which is their future home.

"Grandfather stood and hugged me, holding my head to his chest. 'I hope you can find your way home.' Then he trudged down the hillside and into the lake. As he waded into the healing waters, he turned and waved farewell, and then he was lost in the fog and mist.

"Yes, I found my way home. And I sometimes wake in the night to the sound of strange bird cries, and I wonder if I could find my way back."

JOHNSON GAVE MY SHOULDER a gentle shake. "Wake up, Unegi! It has stopped raining."

And so it had.

Jiggs, My Little Red Rooster

My little red rooster Jiggs crowed all night last night, just as he has done for the past two weeks. Obviously, he isn't interested in announcing sunrise, and I suspect that his cocky adolescent trill has more to do with testosterone than it does with greeting a new day. He is living on my front porch now in one of those Havahart cages. It is cold out there and I have given him a sixty-watt bulb—which might also have something to do with his inability to tell day from night.

I got Jiggs at the Cagle Livestock Exchange over on Hyatt Creek last fall. I had heard about their Saturday morning auctions that specialize in "assorted fowl." My little flock of ancient Brahma hens had been decimated by a fox a few months earlier, so I was hoping to replace them. For those of you that have never attended this incredible event, I recommend it for sheer fun. For three hours I watched an amazing cavalcade of bizarre birds—bantams, guineas, ducks, turkeys, geese, buff Orpingtons, Araucanas, and feather-footed Brahmas squawk and flutter as they are rudely jerked from cages and boxes and held aloft while the auctioneer yodels and croons: "Four fine Plymouth Rocks and a Rhode Island Red Rooster.... What have we got, what have we got.... Say twenty for the batch? Twenty for the batch? Say fifteen? Here we go! I have fifteen.... Do I hear seventeen? No seventeen? Sixteen? Going then, going ... Sold to the man in the red hat for fifteen dollars."

It was fun, but since I'm deaf, I repeatedly failed to bid and missed the Brahma hens. When little terrified Jiggs was plucked from a cage along with an assortment of hens, roosters, and one dove, I not only bid, but I kept bidding and eventually found myself the owner of Jiggs and the whole mismatched collection. At home, I put them all in my little chicken lot and immediately discovered that I had problems. Since Jiggs was the smallest bird in the lot, all of the roosters and even the hens immediately jumped him and flogged him unmercifully. He tried hiding, but they found him. Finally, he flew against the fence with such force that he went through it and vanished into a big thicket above my house, squawking all the way.

Over the next twenty-four hours, I heard poor Jiggs as he wandered aimlessly about the thicket. At some point, he met something that terrified him, and he emerged from the bushes at full tilt and ran into the fence again, ending up inside the lot with his tormenters, who immediately pounced. I guess he decided, like Hamlet, to bear those ills he had, rather than fly to others that might be worse.

In the following weeks, I often found Jiggs standing forlornly outside the lot when I returned home from an errand. When I opened the gate, he would rush inside where he was invariably flogged again. Finally, I asked a friend to help me divide my little lot so I could give Jiggs his own space along with a cute little buff Orpington hen. However, when I settled on the porch to watch the results of my matchmaking, the little hen immediately flogged Jiggs and ran him around the lot until he squeezed through the fence again.

This time I decided to persist. When Jiggs got out, I put him back in and the race continued. Now, at this point, I hadn't given my little red rooster a name, but as I watched him flee from the wrath of that little hen, I recalled the old comic strip, Maggie and Jiggs. In every Sunday serial, the cartoon figure Jiggs, a befuddled, balding little man spent most of his time running from his wife, Maggie, who wielded a mean rolling pin. The name seemed appropriate.

Eventually, some kind of truce was arranged and Jiggs was left to his own devices. After a week, they were roosting together, and finally Jiggs was allowed to scratch beside his paramour . . . wing to wing, you might say. It was then that I heard Jiggs crow for the first time—a little nighttime yodel, tentative and faltering, but a crow nonetheless.

THEN DISASTER STRUCK. I got up one morning to find a black-and-white hawk in my chicken lot. He had already killed everything except a young Brahma rooster, an ancient Brahma hen (who had survived the fox's visit) and Jiggs, who had crawled under the chicken house. The hawk was peering at Jiggs when I appeared, and he reluctantly left, although he didn't go far. While I penned everybody up, bringing Jiggs to the wire cage on the front porch, the hawk watched me from a nearby tree.

So here we are. I am now planning a wire cover for my chicken lot, and Jiggs . . . well, he often cranks his head sideways and peers into the sky above Rhodes Cove. Although I am told that Jiggs's brain is the size of a BB, I am confident that he knows what a hawk is. He is out there some place, that hawk. I'm told that once they find defenseless chickens, they never give up.

Sometimes, when I see tormented teenagers on TV weeping because they are addicted to drugs or are depressed and lonely, I compare their travails to those of Jiggs, my little red rooster.

In the great scheme of things, Jiggs is expendable, I guess. But consider this: He was yanked into a world of loud and meaningless sounds, tormented, abandoned, and rejected. For a brief spell, he snuggled up with his true love, but then some nameless terror descended, murdering his little helpmate and rendering his world a fearful place to be. He tries to hide when migrating birds darken the sky. He is alone and paranoid.

YEAH, HE IS JUST A CHICKEN—a lucky refugee from a Tyson plant—but each time that spunky little fellow gives that bright little trill in the darkness, my heart lifts.

Ode to the Sylva Coffee Shop

Many small mountain towns have a place like the Coffee Shop in Sylva—a café that has become a local landmark. I hopped curb here in 1950 when it had a wooden frame exterior and the jukebox had both "Put Another Nickel In" (Theresa Brewer) and "A Fool Such as I" (Jim Reeves). At night, the parking lot was always full of World War II veterans in souped-up cars. Sylva was "wet" and life was good. Just up the street, the Ritz had just started showing Sunday movies and I never missed a Cagney, Mitchum, or Bogart. I got my salary docked every Sunday because I insisted on seeing the final fifteen minutes of the movie before I came to work for Cicero Bryson. I would stand in the back of the theater with the door open, and when the credits started sliding down the screen, I would run like hell.

Now, sixty years later, the Coffee Shop has morphed into a kind of nostalgia museum where you can eat breakfast, lunch, and dinner under the benevolent stares of John Wayne, Clint Eastwood, Dale Earnhardt, and the Three Stooges. There are James Dean, Bogart, Elvis, and Marilyn frolicking in period shots of drive-in café parking lots and all-night restaurants (a parody of Edward Hopper's *Nighthawks*), their images interspersed with vintage Coca-Cola signs, Uneeda Biscuits ads, and hundreds of personalized license plates with every state (and Aruba!) accounted for. Advertisements for fresh strawberry pie sit cheek to jowl with a seating section labeled "Police Officer Parking." A collection of vintage pop bottles (Sunspot, Grapette) mingle with potted plants and birdhouses. Johnny Cash, a photo of the Brothers of the Bush (1950s Centennial), and a photo of Popcorn Sutton. The sheer magnitude of this display causes visitors to stand, mouth agape, staring at the walls, while the constant clatter of spatulas, the sizzle of butter, bacon, hamburger, and the shouts of the breakfast crew mingle in a kind of grand, roaring symphony of sound, smells, and color.

The majority of the Coffee Shop patrons are local. Elderly couples eat dinner here and the daily menu reflects local preferences: fried okra, cabbage, meatloaf, trout, slaw, potato salad. A number of Cherokees eat here regularly. And then there are the Western Carolina college students who often stare about as they eat as though they had found themselves in an exotic, primitive village in Russia or Germany.

But the Coffee Shop endures, a primal life form that simply acquires an additional layer of scales and armor: a protective coating of history and pop stars, Uneeda Biscuits and Coke—a shield that deflects the changing world.

Things Have Been Bad, But...

One of my most enduring memories of my grandparents concerns a ritual that they performed on summer evenings in Rhodes Cove. Settling into two ancient rocking chairs on the front porch, they would watch the Balsam Mountains fade in the twilight while they gently rocked, talking in a subdued monotone about the condition of the world.

"The town cut them big water oaks down along Scott's Creek yesterday," says my grandfather.

"They hush your mouth," says my grandmother. (She didn't mean for my grandfather to stop talking. That was just one of her favorite expressions of surprise or dismay.)

"Them trees have been there for sixty years."

"Well, why in the world did they do that?"

"Power lines, I think. They are running more 'lectricity into the Cove."

"That's progress, I reckon."

My grandfather snorted. "Is that what you call it?" Then, he would give a heartfelt sigh and say, "Things have been bad, but they are going to get worse."

My grandmother would nod. "Ain't nothing we can do about it."

When I was a teenager, sitting on that dark porch listening to the sound of shelled peas dropping in counterpoint to the rasp of a whetstone while my grandparents repeated that sad refrain, I sometimes ground my teeth with frustration. Why were they so damned passive? All of that stoic acceptance bothered me. Why didn't they raise hell? When I gave little rants about the democratic process, petitions, and civil disobedience (a phrase I had learned from Henry David Thoreau), they would look at each other and smile. When the "powers that be" chose to tear down most of Sylva's notable landmarks, including the depot, the Candler house, the high school, and the Ritz Theater, I heard that irksome refrain, "Things have been bad . . ." blending with ". . . nothing we can do about it." A familiar world was being erased around us and being replaced by glass and steel.

In the years after my grandparents passed away, I sometimes uncovered surprising bits of information about their lives before I came to live with them. According to one of my grandfather's cronies, he had opposed the expansion of the town's city limits sixty years ago and had made his feelings clear at town board meetings. I also learned that my grandparents had abandoned the "town church" when they came to feel that it resembled a social club; they then joined a rural church where they felt more comfortable. Perhaps they couldn't change the mad rush toward the future, but they could refuse to participate.

Things began to add up. A janitor at Western Carolina University once told me how my grandfather had stepped between a bunch of sullen drunks at a local service station and the janitor, who was then a frightened African American teenager on his way home late at night. "They would have hurt me bad, if it hadn't been for your grandfather," who had started telling jokes to distract the drunks. My grandfather had never mentioned the incident. Another crony told me about when my grandfather used to "buy votes"—a practice that made me ashamed when I first heard it. "It's not what you think," the man said. "When your grandfather had offered to 'buy votes' in Rhodes Cove for the Democratic Party, he simply took the money and bought groceries for all of the poorest families in the Cove. In all likelihood, they would have all voted a straight Democratic ticket anyway."

So, my grandparents did not protest or write letters to the editor of the local paper. Instead they persisted in quietly living lives and making personal decisions that were in direct opposition to the march of progress. They continued to farm and struggled to keep a host of family traditions and customs alive, customs like family reunions and "Decoration Day." I guess they knew that the tide was against them and that in time their way of life would be plowed under or swept away.

I am still living in my grandparents' old farmhouse, and when I sit on my front porch in the evening, the Cove is full of dust, the sound of machinery, and the smell of burned oil and gasoline. Water and sewer lines are crawling through the Cove. I hear talk of wondrous plans. Condominiums and high-rise apartments in the Cove! I still have a few chickens and a fragment of a garden, but the concrete keeps creeping forward and the chainsaws are getting louder. Progress is here!

I GUESS IT IS time to go. Lots of my neighbors are gone already, searching for another remote cove where the fog comes down in the evening and the rain crows mourn at night, a place where they can still have a garden and pick up their mail from a roadside mailbox without fear of being run down by traffic. Some have sold out to the enemy and have moved to town, where I sometimes see them driving aimlessly about or talking to each other on cell phones as they wander through Walmart.

Evenings on the porch, I sit with the ghosts of my grandparents and we slowly rock, watching the Balsam Mountains fade in the twilight.

"Things have been bad . . ." says my grandfather.

"Nothing we can do about it," says my grandmother.

Then they laugh, for that was their nature.

"Did you feed the chickens?" says my grandfather.

"Time to milk the cow," says my grandmother. And they rise and shuffle off to complete those time-honored errands that have marked their daily lives for almost a century. It is a ritual that they will repeat until they, too, and all they held dear fades in the twilight.

The Pink Radio

When I was five years old, my uncle Stoogie won a pink radio at the Cherokee Fair and he gave it to me. He told me he was worried about me because I stayed in my bedroom all the time reading funny books (most of them were not funny but wonderful). My bedroom had been my uncle Albert's bedroom, but with the coming of World War II, he joined the Navy and I moved from the old couch in the living room to the dark, chilly bedroom in the back of the house.

My grandparents were ill prepared to raise a quirky little kid. They grieved for my father's death for years, and in the meanwhile I was in the back room with nothing for companionship except a huge stack of funny books. I stayed there in that dark room much of the time. I spent more time with Sub-mariner, Captain Marvel, Superman, and Plastic Man than I did with other kids because other kids were rare.

And when Uncle Stoogie came to see me—he said he had promised my Momma that he would—he was upset. I was pale and sickly, not to mention shy. So he said that we were going to the Cherokee Indian Fair, and he dragged me out of that dark room and we got in his car and drove to Cherokee . . . which for me was like visiting a foreign country.

I was fascinated by Uncle Stoogie in his Air Force uniform that was loaded with brass and medals. He had a scar on his cheek that looked like he had pressed a Coke bottle cap against the flesh until it left that scar and he chewed Dentine and grinned and asked me a thousand questions. We smelled the Cherokee Indian Fair for two miles before we got there! It was hot dogs and fried sausage and cotton candy and that smell hung in the chill, October night over the Indian Fair like a cloud.

There were Cherokees camped out on blankets and quilts around the fairgrounds, and you could hear the Ferris wheel and the merry-go-round, and I ate three hot dogs and rode the swings and threw up and then ate three more hot dogs. We fished little wooden fish with numbers on their backs from a tin tube of rushing water and won a stuffed cat and we threw darts at balloons and shot rifles at metal ducks that fell with a CLACK when I hit them and then, finally, we played bingo. That is when Uncle Stoogie told me, "You see that pink radio on the top shelf? I am going to win that for you."

Now, when I look back on that night, I guess I realize that Uncle Stoogie was drunk, but I didn't know what drunk was, so we played and we played and we won a big blanket but we never got close to winning that radio until Uncle Stoogie just got out his billfold and told that carny, "How much for that goddamned pink radio?!" And suddenly I had it. On the way home with my pink radio in my lap, Uncle Stoogie said, "Hey kid . . ." Yeah, he talked like that. Sorta like James Cagney. He said, "We are just beginning."

WHEN WE GOT TO my grandparents' home, he knocked down two rows of corn turning his car around, and then he said, "I'll see you in the morning," and I didn't know what that meant, but the next morning he woke me up. He said, "Come on, kid." And the next thing I knew, he had me unrolling a huge wheel of copper wire and we strung an antenna from my bedroom window all the way to the top of Painter Knob, ran it on little white insulators, and then from Painter Knob back to the barn, and when we surveyed our creation that winked in the sun and whistled in the wind, he roughed my hair up and said, "Now, kid, we are going to listen to Russians and Chinese and Eskimos!"

It was dark before he was done, but then he plugged that radio in and hooked it up and SHAZAM! That radio was like a great pink nightlight, and we sat on my bed and turned that tuner knob that sang and wept and squealed. It was wonderful . . . there was music and sirens and people jabbering and orchestras and a quartet singing, "You better get Wildroot Cream Oil, Charlie," and a laughing man who said, "From high atop the downtown Rose Room in Chicago, we bring you, *Tommy Tucker Time!*" Then there was a husky-voiced woman who whispered, "Are you lonesome out there tonight, Big Boy? Well, this is your gal Sal and I am here to keep you company." And then she sang songs about being alone at night and somewhere in her serenade, Uncle Stoogie said, "Well, kid, I'll leave you to it." And he was gone and I lay in the pink-tinted darkness and listened to the voices singing and shouting and sometimes I slept, but always, I would wake to find my room singing to me.

UNCLE STOOGIE IS LONG GONE—he ended up as croupier in Las Vegas. But I owe him a thousand nights of *Let's Pretend* and *The Inner Sanctum* and "Roma Wines brings you *Suspense*" and Arthur Godfrey singing "The Blue Ridge Mountains of Virginia" and then the Shadow laughed and said, "The Shadow knows!" I swapped Clark Kent for Lamont Cranston and learned to sing all the words to "Hear That Lonesome Whistle Blow." There was a quartet that sang, "Turn the radio on and listen to the music in the air" . . . and I did.

Billy Condon

I am thinking of those classmates who vanished from my life. They simply appeared one morning and struggled to survive in my classroom and then something happened and they vanished. Perhaps some of my peers know what happened to them.

For one, there was Sidney Quiet. That was his real name. The teachers called him an albino, and he had off-color eyes. Was he "retarded?" I don't know. He wasn't angry or destructive, but he sometimes did alarming things that were meant to please us. He was larger than the other students, awkward, and very strong. He often followed a group of us kids during recess, and in time we learned that he would do anything we asked. ("We" was usually one of my peers.)

We were then in school in the First Baptist Church because our elementary school building had been condemned. Our teachers simply read us a statement from the superintendent's office and told us to report to the church on Monday and our teachers would take us to our new "classroom." It was a strange day as we climbed the stairs to large rooms where our teachers waited. The rooms were so large, they became the classroom to more than one grade. The teachers divided the room with a ribbon, and the fifth grade was on one side of the ribbon and the sixth grade on the other. When the teachers began talking, calling the rolls, and actually teaching, the noise level was incredible ... a kind of Tower of Babel as we listened to a chapter of Tom Sawyer and a chapter of our geography book about the Tigris and the Euphrates Rivers at the same time.

The teachers were obviously at a loss as to how to make this new building work, so we had a lot of study halls while the teachers whispered to each other in the kitchen. I sat with Charlie K., my best friend, and Charlie had already discovered that the church had a heating system with large metal ducts, large enough to take Charlie, who had already crawled from our room to the auditorium. He had plans to "escape" each day and bewilder the teachers—he was absent at roll call but present an hour later.

We returned to the old condemned elementary school building each day to eat lunch. On the first day, as we were struggling down the packed stairwell, Charlie K. became exasperated and called out to Sidney Quiet, "Sidney, can you clear the way down these steps?" Sidney, eager to please, grabbed Avalene Allen and hoisted her over his head and threw her down the stairs. Avalene hit a dozen students and sent them all careening down the steps where they crashed into the hall doors. Amazingly, no one was seriously hurt, but they all lay in a shocked and tangled mess of arms and legs. Charlie K. looked up to find Sidney staring at him, waiting for a response. "I was kidding," said Charlie, dismayed. Sidney looked disappointed, and his large hands opened and closed in frustration. "Thank you, Sidney," Charlie said in a whisper.

All of the students finally managed to get up and stumble down the stairs ... all except Avalene Allen, who had lost her shoes and was crawling back up them. "Did you see that?" said Charlie. "Picked her up and threw her down the steps like she weighed ten pounds." I noticed that Sidney was standing behind him, like an obedient servant waiting for the next request. Charlie finally noticed Sidney and said, "Everything is fine, Sidney." Sidney wandered away and life went on as usual.

Then, one morning, Tommy Morris, the kid who had a father who owned a camp on Lake Glenville, made the mistake of shoving Sidney. "Get out of my way, Dummie," he said. Sidney slowly picked Tommy up and slammed him on the ground, and then sat on him. Tommy was bewildered and he began to flail Sidney with one hand, saying, "Do you give up?" That was kind of funny since Tommy's blows were weak and Sidney decided to choke him and he began to turn blue. I called to Charlie K. and said, "Make him stop." Abruptly, Sidney stopped on his own. I don't know why, but he did. He got off of Tommy and wandered away.

I asked Charlie why Sidney lost interest in choking Tommy. "I don't know," he said. "I am not Sidney's keeper." I don't know what happened after that, but the following morning Sidney didn't get off the bus that ran from Gateway to the school. The teachers whispered a bit and Miss Geisler said something about "Sidney's fits" and that perhaps he had one and had to be kept home. I never saw Sidney again. Charlie K. was relieved.

Then there was an angry boy named Kimsey who carried a hawkbill knife in his hand when we went outside for recess. He would punch a kid and show him the knife in his hand. "Don't mess with me," he would say. We didn't mess with him. In fact, we stayed away from him, often leaving him to stand alone on the playground. We had a new principal named Hare who called Kimsey out in the hall and asked him for the knife. Kimsey said, "Don't mess with me." Then Kimsey vanished. Where did he go?

Then the quiet boy showed up. His name was Billy Condon and he sat in the last seat in the back of the room. Every time I looked at him, he would smile and nod, but he never spoke. I asked Charlie K. about him. "I asked him who he was," Charlie said, "and he said his name was not Condon, but he was told to answer to it. He said his real name was Carden. Like yours." Then, one morning he was gone. Vanished like all the others.

I did see him again many years later, when I was a teenager and sometimes went to Asheville with a cousin named Ed Henson. We would drink beer and drive aimlessly around. All that changed one day when Ed came to Cherokee and picked me up.

When I got in the car, Ed said, "And the boy in the back seat you already know." I turned and spoke to the guy in the back seat and, lo, it was Billy Condon! He smiled, just as he always had. Then I asked Ed to take me home since I had left a ten-dollar bill in my other pants.

At the turn-off to my house on 107, Ed pulled off the road and said, "Billy, I guess you need to wait on us. Stay here and we will be right back."

I was bewildered. I said, "He can go with us."

Billy smiled and got out of the car. "I'll wait right here," he said.

On the way to the house, Ed said, "What is wrong with you? You know we can't take him with us to your house." At that point, I got a feeling that everyone knew something that I didn't. The only way I could find out what they knew was to shut up and listen.

So I said, "Yeah, I forgot."

"Forgot!" said Ed. "Damn, so you remember now. Is that right?"

I apologized, and on we went.

We drove to Asheville to a restaurant called The Three Pigs, and I sat and stared at Billy Condon. "Where did you go when you left school?" I asked.

Billy smiled and said, "My mother took a job in Washington, so we moved." Then he said that he was in school in Chapel Hill. He started talking about music and a band that he played with, and I was bewildered.

Who are you, Billy Condon?

Sadie Womack

I am not even sure of her name. I was five or six when she showed up one afternoon while I was sitting on the porch with

Grandpa. I was staring down the little dusty trail that ran past our house when she appeared, looking like something out of the Old Testament . . . a tall figure with a staff walking slowly. She halted now and then and stood for a moment, surveying the world around her. Then, she prodded the dirt and took several more steps. Now and then, she spit. A snuff-dipper! She was old, and her face was withered like a prune.

"Who is that, Grandpa?"

He put down his whetstone and leaned forward peering at this old woman creeping up the trail. He stood up and went to the end of the porch for a better view.

"Well, if it isn't Sadie Womack." Grandpa smiled and said, "She's coming here."

"How do you know?"

"Well, GarNell, she has been here before. She usually stays a week, and then she goes over to East Sylva to Aster Plemmons, and then to Floyd's . . . and sometimes somebody takes her to Cowee, where there are a dozen folks she can visit." By the time Sadie reached our porch, Grandpa had told my grandmother that we had a visitor . . . and had told me an incredible story.

IT SEEMED THAT SADIE was a homeless old woman who had been rejected by her family. She was totally dependent on the goodwill of others, and over the years a kind of network of folks had developed around her. However, there was another story that most of Sadie's friends knew. Sadie had not been rejected by her family. She had a home and had spent her life working. After becoming a widow, she had taken on the job of tending the cow and chickens and managed to provide for her family. She had lived a grim existence for all of her life. Grandpa said that when she was seventy, she had invited her children to dinner and then she had announced her "retirement." She presented them with the deed to her property and told them she had decided to enjoy life for the remainder of her time on Earth.

I was not sure I understood why people willingly accepted Sadie, and moreover seemed to be pleased to have her. But then, I hadn't heard Sadie talk. After she had eaten a healthy meal, we sat at the table and listened as she talked about where she had been and what she had seen. She was an encyclopedia of gossip: she knew the births, deaths, divorces of three counties, and she remembered most of the old families of our region. She knew "lost" recipes, and she remembered all of the fights and murders. She could sing in a fine tenor all of the old gospel songs, including "Signs and Wonders." She told me several haint tales that scared me. Sadie was "entertainment."

The next day, Sadie sat on the porch with my grandmother, and, as they shelled peas and shucked corn, she talked. As I mentioned, she dipped snuff and seeing her spit was a marvel. She could nail a fly or a spider from ten feet. I had never seen a snuff-spitter who was a markswoman. When she scored a hit, she would wink at me. I think her victims lived, but I suspect that their worldview was altered.

SHE STAYED A WEEK and left one morning, on her way to East Sylva, where the Plemmons family was expecting her. I watched her out of sight, that tall old lady with the big staff. I already missed her. She frequently showed up in my dreams, and after I began to tell stories, I often thought of Sadie's journey through the lives of others. I often now think that the fate of a storyteller could be a never-ending adventure if we all followed Sadie's example. I guess the wheelchair that I live in now would limit my opportunities, but still . . .

Booger

I found Booger at the coffee shop some fifteen years ago—a tiny kitten with only one eye open, and although I could easily cover her with one hand, I couldn't muffle the anguished MEEOOW! that she produced. It was like the cry of some tortured soul in hell, filled with equal parts despair and terror. She had matted, multicolored fur, and when I cupped her to the shoulder of my jacket, she sank her tiny claws deep into the fabric and clung there like a small wad of Velcro. Something had plucked her from a bleak and uncertain fate and she had no intention of letting go.

I opened the back door of the Coffee Shop and caught the eye of the short-order cook at the grill. "Is it okay if I take this kitten?"

The cook laughed. "Are you kidding? That screech was getting on my nerves."

So Booger came home with me. She only stopped giving her heartbroken lamentation when I pried her off my jacket and forced her mouth into a saucer of milk. I think she underwent a kind of instant weaning. Then she slept in my pocket the rest of the day, emitting a loud, rumbling purr . . . a sound that, like her cry of distress, was unusually loud for such a small creature.

There was a major problem with Booger's becoming a part of my household—Jack, my Jack Russell. However, I thought I had a solution. Booger would be a barn cat. I would create a perfect environment in my old abandoned barn, complete with food, an old tattered blanket, and an endless supply of mice. But when I deposited Booger in her new home, she was immediately unhappy, emitting a yodel of misery that followed me back to the house. I told myself that she would adjust, and I would come each day with Friskies and love.

It didn't work, of course. When I returned the following day, Booger was gone. I searched through the saw briar and broom sage around the barn, leaving food and milk in the old feedroom. After three days, I gave up hoping that she had found her way to a neighbor's house where she was now warm and content. I found—or heard—her a week later in the old garden, covered with beggar lice and terrified. It took me several hours to clean her up, tugging each sticky burr from her fur while she continued to give that anguished cry. Although she endued the "cleansing," she obviously considered the ordeal a personal attack. I don't think she ever forgave me for that.

Eventually, we worked out a living arrangement. Booger lived in the attic and since Jack was afraid of steps, she was beyond his reach. Although she left each day, vanishing into the dense woods above my old farmhouse, she returned each night, exploding through Jack's doggie door in the bathroom and racing to the top of the stairs, where she sat giving Jack and me a baleful stare. Obviously, we were not to be trusted. She only visited her food dish after we were in the bed. We lived like that for over ten years.

TWO YEARS AGO, I decided to give up my old farmhouse. The roof was leaking and I had passed several uncomfortable winters there due to the absence of insulation and dependable heat. I was fortunate enough to qualify for an apartment in a community complex that catered to the poor and elderly. Jack went with me (although he had to pay rent too), and we suddenly found ourselves basking in well-heated rooms complete with a dishwasher and a garbage disposal. However, Booger remained in the old farmhouse. There was no place in my new community for a maladjusted kitty.

As fall turned to winter, I worried about the woolly Booger that lived in the attic. Although I had cut off the heat and electricity, I went by each day and left food in Booger's dish. Within a month, the house was filled with cobwebs, mold, and mildew. When the first snow came, Booger abandoned the attic and moved to the front porch. In time, I came to realize that she was waiting for me. I hadn't heard that banshee wail in several years, but now it returned. Each day, as I trudged through the snow, Booger greeted me with loud recriminations. She had been abandoned again.

I guess guilt did me in. More and more, I had misgivings about Booger's fate and as I listened to that anguished wail each day, it came to be a mix of both despair and accusation.

"Where have you been?" she seemed to say. As the house became increasingly bleak and inhospitable, the cold, empty rooms filled with dust devils and little tumbleweeds composed of Booger's fur. I made a decision. I turned the electricity on and hooked up a heating pad for Booger to sleep on. I discovered that if I stayed a while, my old cat became less fretful. I brought books to read, and a radio that picked up an FM station in Asheville. One night, I dozed off in my chair and woke to find Booger in my lap, her mournful meow reduced to a vibrating purr, like an idling engine or a car.

And so I came home. Despite the protests and advice of my friends, I talked them into loading my battered belongings and making the trek back to Rhodes Cove. Several old acquaintances helped me clean the old house, remove the mildew, and fire up the wood stove. Jack was obviously pleased, and we are now gradually rediscovering the pleasures of familiar things—the little stream in the front yard, the rain crows on the ridge above the house. It is time to put chickens back in the empty lot and plant tomatoes in the garden.

Did I come home because of my old cat, Booger? Well, that would make me some kind of fool, wouldn't it? But it is gratifying to see Jack and Booger asleep in the same chair, their noses buried in each other's fur. Each night, Jack burrows beneath the quilts on my bed and Booger sleeps on my pillow, where she can keep watch on the silent fields and the night sky through the window. After all of those years of glaring at us from the attic steps, she has finally managed to insinuate herself into our lives.

Sometimes, I think it is the other way around—that Jack and I have finally managed to sneak into Booger's world. When I stay up late reading and listening to music, I sometimes see Booger in the dark kitchen, where she lays on her back purring. She is a chubby cat now after so many years of painful thinness. She rocks slowly back and forth, shifting from left to right in a kind of an ecstasy of contentment. Then she will explode, vaulting to her feet and racing away up to the attic, down and out of the house, leaving the "doggie door" clattering, and then back to the kitchen where she sits and washes a foot, her huge green eyes watching me. It took me a while to realize that Booger is ... playing. And more than that, she is celebrating.

My Grandfather and Jesse James

Back in the 1940s when popular movies used to return each year, my grandparents waited each summer for their favorites. *How Green Was My Valley* and *Sergeant York* were my grandmother's favorites, and she also loved *Trail of the Lonesome Pine* (the color version with Fred MacMurray, Sylvia Sidney, and Henry Fonda). However, the big family favorite was Tyrone Power in *Jesse James*.

When *Jesse James* came around, I remember we dressed like we were going to church and walked from Rhodes Cove to the Ritz Theater. By the time I was twelve, I knew most of the lines and all of the characters in this lurid saga, but that didn't diminish my enjoyment. (I usually had my cap pistol concealed in my Sunday school coat ... just in case.) Due to the popularity of the movie, there were several sequels, including *The Return of Frank James* with Henry Fonda. However, although my grandfather admired the vengeful brother, his heart belonged to Jesse.

My grandfather was an excitable man and would sometimes talk back to the characters on the screen. He hated Bob Ford, the man who killed Jesse, and often yelled insults at him. In the famous scene in which Jesse climbs onto a chair in order to straighten a picture on the wall, thereby giving Bob Ford the opportunity to shoot him in the back, my grandfather would jump to his feet and yell, "Look out, Jesse! Look out!" I wonder now if he hoped to save Jesse ... hoped that Jesse would turn and see that "dirty little coward that shot Mr. Howard" and blow him to Kingdom Come. ("Mr. Howard" was the name that Jesse was living under at the time of his death.)

On the way home my grandfather would expound on the significance of Jesse's tragedy, invariably noting that he was the victim of the callous and immoral "sonsabitches that run this country." He would caution me to be on the lookout, and he warned, "Sooner or later, you are going to meet them." He was talking about a government in cahoots with the major industries in this country such as the railroads, the TVA, and the folks that "run our people out of the Smokies." Later, in the darkness of our front porch as we sat listening to the night sounds in Rhodes Cove, he would continue and usually end up singing a few verses from a ballad about Pretty Boy Floyd:

> Now as through this world I ramble,
> I see lots of funny men
> Some will rob you with a six gun,
> And some with a fountain pen
>
> But as through your life you travel,
> As through your life you roam
> You won't never see an outlaw,
> Drive a family from their home.

But my grandfather's empathy with outlaws and his grievances with the government and our legal system went much deeper than movies and ballads. He had lost a son, a gifted musician, my father, to a drunk with a rusty pistol. Although brought to trial and sentenced, the drunkard's family launched a vigorous campaign to get him released from prison. My grandfather countered with a campaign to keep him there. In the end my grandfather lost, even though he had sold most of his land to pay the lawyers. He wanted that broken little drunk punished, and yes, he wanted him dead. Devious lawyers, politics, and the value of the mountain land that the little drunk's father owned—all of this deprived my grandfather of the justice he wanted.

When I was eight years old, I remember an afternoon when the local sheriff came to tell my grandfather that the convicted killer had been released from a prison in Raleigh that morning. "Don't do nothing foolish, Arthur," he said. "Let it go." Then, he added, "He won't be living in this county anyway." As we watched Sheriff Middleton walk back down the trail, my grandfather wept.

After a while, he straightened in his chair, and said, "Well, what do we have here? What kind of justice is this?" Pointing at me, he said, "What I see is an orphan young'en, two poverty-stricken farmers (meaning himself and the family of the killer), and two rich lawyers." Then he gave a bitter laugh and said, "I guess the only justice that we get in this life is what we get for ourselves."

So it was that in time, my grandfather came to admire outlaws. I think that he saw them as his advocates—courageous individuals who refused to suffer passively, men who attempted to rectify the wrongs suffered by the poor and defenseless. My grandfather spent the majority of his life in hard manual labor, weeding, hoeing, milking, chopping. These were chores that continued after darkness had fallen and began each morning before daylight. However, sitting in the dark of the Ritz Theater, I saw him transformed as he experienced the thrill of robbing the Glendale train.

Eventually, I discovered that my grandfather was not alone. While working in Haywood, Swain, and Macon Counties, I often heard others speak bitterly of injustices: the destruction of Hazel Creek by the Ritter Lumber Company, the building of Fontana Dam, and the governmentally sanctioned eviction of mountain families in Cataloochee and all the coves and valleys of what would become known as the Great Smoky Mountains National Park.

I know that these people shared my grandfather's admiration for outlaws, and Hollywood knew it too, for young criminals seemed to be everywhere. If not Jesse, Pretty Boy Floyd, and Billy the Kid, then Henry Fonda in *Trail of the Lonesome Pine* and finally Robert Mitchum in *Thunder Road*—a film that played to packed houses for two decades.

NOW, SIXTY YEARS LATER, I remember my grandfather's warning about the powerful, greedy entities: "Sooner or later, you are going to meet them." I have, but instead of Pinkertons, railroads, and robber barons, I have encountered Duke Energy and Visa and AT&T, and I feel as powerless as my grandfather did. I am also hoping that there is someone out there who will be my advocate; someone who can strike fear into the heart of the arrogant and powerful.

Are you out there, Jesse?

Gun Trade

My grandfather loved guns. I remember that he used to hold what were called "gun swaps" on our front porch and people would come from all over the Cove. They would bring guns wrapped in oil-soaked blankets and lay them out on the porch along with sweet-smelling oils and lubricants.

Sometimes, they would pick up a rifle or a shotgun, always with an oily rag in their hands, always polishing, wiping away fingerprints from the blue metal and stocks and they would pull bolts and levers, listening to the slide and click of all of those parts. That seemed to be a part of the experience, I guess, listening to way those parts slid and clicked into place. There were Mossbergs and Colts and Smith & Wessons, and mean-looking little pistols called Owl's Heads. There were always some old pros who could do things like strike matches or drive nails from twenty yards away. There were hunters, too, but now when I look back on those long evenings that stretched on into the night with porch lights and oil lamps, the majority of those men (and yeah, they were all men) weren't hunters (or robbers and killers), they were men who loved the heft and the slick click and the mechanical action of a piece of machinery that they could take apart and put together in minutes.

The first time that I used my grandfather's rifle to shoot an English sparrow off a wire, I was stunned by what I had done, at how I had transformed that cunning little creature that flew and sang into a limp and shattered bit of flesh that I held in my hand as its warmth faded. I lost all interest in killing birds.

The men would talk, exchanging stories that involved guns and marksmanship and death. Mostly, they were friends and they attended the same churches, family reunions, and socials and worked in the same mills and stores. Hunting was restricted mostly to squirrels and rabbits. Also, swapping was not restricted to pistols and rifles. Some of those men came with fiddles or guitars. They sometimes even bartered cows and mules and I remember the night my grandfather swapped our little Swiss cow for a Mossburg repeating rifle. Many times, men came and left without swapping anything at all . . . it was like they had joined in a ritual that was uplifting and reaffirming.

WHEN I WAS EIGHT I went through a bad patch. I was a scrawny little kid, inept and awkward (except in my imagination), and I became a kind of sacrificial victim to a couple of vicious brutes that terrorized the rest of us. There was Avery who liked to smack me till my nose bled. Then there was Kenny who was fat and liked to sit astride of me while Avery pitched my books through the window of the school bus into the briar patches along the road in Rhodes Cove. They did it every day. The roads in Rhodes Cove were crooked and sort of uncoiled in big loops, so when I was trying to get my sweater out of the patch, I could see Avery and Kenny walking home and they always called to me, laughing, "See you tomorrow."

So there came an afternoon when I said, enough. I ran to the house and opened the closet where my grandfather kept the Mossberg. It wasn't loaded, so I had to find shells. I found two. My grandmother heard me and saw me slide those shells into the Mossberg. What are you doing, GarNell? Suddenly, I was clever and quick-thinking.

"There is a big rat in the front yard," I said.

When I raced to the end of the porch, there were Avery and Kenny up the hill, laughing and throwing rocks that were bouncing off the tin roof of our barn. When I found Avery in the sights, I paused and then fired at a point just above Avery's head. The distance was enough to require a drop . . . When I fired, Avery fell like a sack of potatoes. I swung to fat Kenny and fired. He went down. My honest reaction was relief. Tomorrow, they would not be on the bus. But then I saw the broom sage move and Avery and Kenny crawled across the road and ran for home.

A LOT OF REMARKABLE THINGS happened pretty rapidly after that. The local sheriff came and parked in the driveway. My grandfather went out and got in the sheriff's car and they talked a long time. Then my grandfather came and got the Mossburg, gave me a look of alarm and took the gun to the sheriff. The sheriff went away and my grandfather came and sat on the porch for a long time, staring at me. Finally, he said, "GarNell, you can't kill people just because they piss you off."

I answered, "Why not? You told me that the only justice you get in life is what you get yourself."

"Well . . . maybe I was wrong about that." After a moment, he said, "Did you mean to kill them boys?"

"I don't know. I aimed high since it was so far."

"Kenny claims that he lost a patch of hair."

"No kidding!" Fat Kenny lost some hair. He had been my friend before Avery came along.

THE NEXT DAY AT SCHOOL, I met Avery and Kenny in the hall. They turned around and went the other way. That afternoon, they weren't on the bus. I was pleased. I was also impressed by the power of guns. I'm not saying that I did the right thing, but I was a kid. I still wonder if I meant to kill Avery and Kenny. I honestly don't know, but I am pleased that they vanished from my life.

My mother, Irene.

My father, "Happy" Carden.

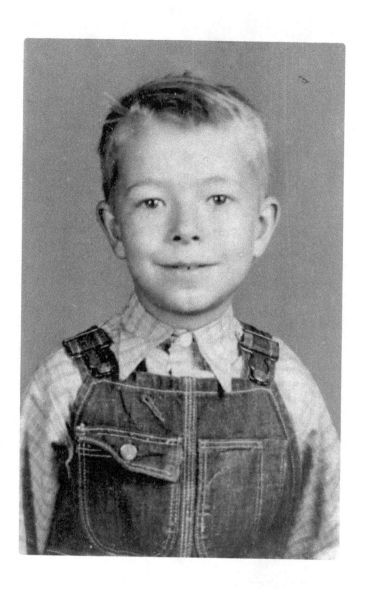

Back in elementary school.

Me and my grandparents.

My grandfather, Arthur Carden, and his Esso truck.

Tiny.

The Carden family at my great-grandmother's house in Cowee.

Mountain Water as Religion

Kind hearts, I have been thinking about water, and I can say with certainty that water once had a role in my grandparents' life that was near to a religion. In the world where I once lived, water was at the heart of everything. Every household had either a well or a spring, and I loved to open the little door on my grandfather's spring where lizards scurried across the bottom of the water, stirring up sand and, according to my grandfather, kept "the spring water pure." When we visited the Plemmons family, I could let down the bucket in the well and listen to that awesome, magnified sound of water drops falling into the darkness. My grandfather had a water system that consisted of hollow pine logs fitted together and bringing cold spring water to our back porch where my grandmother's butter and eggs and milk sat in a trough filled with continually running water, where I once kept a live trout, and where, each night, my grandfather stood with a gourd dipper and drank his fill.

Gone now. All of that magic was going, even then.

When my grandfather drove that oil truck up Glenville Mountain or to the rock crusher in Little Canada, there were places where he would pull over and get his tin dipper out of the glove compartment and disappear into the undergrowth to where he and a multitude of others knew there was an unpolluted spring. Often the water was running from a pipe driven into a rock bed and the water sprang from that pipe in a steady stream. Oftentimes, there was a Garrett Sweet Snuff glass jar atop of a stake or a gourd and the water was crystal clear and ice cold because it had filtered through rock and tree roots, and my grandfather would stand reverently drinking a kind of water that was even then becoming a rarity. Each time the roadbed was rebuilt and each time construction work uprooted a water system buried in the mountainside, another crick vanished.

Twenty years ago, a county agent told me there was no longer such a thing as an unpolluted well or spring. Tree roots did in my grandfather's unique water system, and finally water tests indicated that even the old springs (guarded by spring lizards) were contaminated. I bowed to the Gods of Progress and got "city water."

So, on we go, kind hearts. Progress is coming to Rhodes Cove. On the mountain above me, I used to flush grouse and pheasant, which would rise like thunder and scare me badly. Now, there is only silent timber, abandoned springs, and the distant sound of traffic. Pavement and streetlights creep closer each day.

ONE OF MY RECURRING DREAMS is of my grandfather, rising from his bed at two o'clock in the morning and walking barefoot through the house to get a drink of water. Sometimes I would peer from my bedroom at him standing there in the moonlight in his long johns, drinking from that long-handled gourd dipper, and halting now and again to whisper, "Ah, Booyz, that's good." I never knew what "Booyz" meant, but both of my grandparents said it. It expressed a profound pleasure. When my grandmother died in the hospital, the nurse brought a washcloth dipped in ice water to her room and washed her face. My grandmother smiled. "Does that feel good, Mrs. Carden?"

My grandmother replied, "Ah, Booyz, it does."

Coffins in the Flood

Looking back on my childhood, there were hundreds of nights that I remember sitting on the porch with my grandparents. This was before streetlights and pavement came to Rhodes Cove. The night was filled with the sound of my grandfather's whetstone as he sat on the steps sharpening his mowing scythes, reap hooks, and hoes. However, after my father was murdered, my grandfather often retreated to the barn where he spent hours hulling walnuts. It is a filthy job, but it seemed to suit my grandfather's brooding and sadness. Sometimes he stayed in the loft of the barn with a lantern all night, and now I saw my grandmother look toward the barn and the faint glow of the lantern. My grandmother rocked in her cane-bottomed rocker and snapped beans and shelled peas, and the sound of the beans and peas dropping into her tin wash pan had a measured regularity. There were night birds and crickets and the occasional mournful sound of rain crows from Painter Knob. When my grandfather added a single electric porch light that gave a gentle glow to the scene, we gained the flutter and buzz of "pinch bugs," drawn by the light and always falling to the porch floor where our two cats waited. The conflicts were brief and violent.

We rarely spoke, but when my grandmother stopped stringing and snapping, it was usually a cue that she was about to speak. "It is going to rain tonight," she said.

"How do you know?" I said, hoping to create a dialogue with my grandmother.

"There is a circle around the moon," she said.

"Was Grandpa your only boyfriend?" I blurted out, eager to get her to talk. My grandmother laughed, and stared at me for a moment.

"No, GarNell, I had a bunch of boyfriends before Arthur showed up."

"Were any of them serious competition?" There was a long silence and my grandmother stared into the darkness.

"There was one feller who was sort of a dandy. Fancy dresser. His name was Jason Ensley. The only man I ever knew with that name. Jason."

"So, what happened to him?"

"He died in the big cholera epidemic that came through the mountains when I was a teenager."

"Did he live in Big Ridge?"

"No, he lived in Sylva, but he traveled. He was some kind of salesman. But he took me to church for a while."

"Did you like him?"

My grandmother gave a little snort, and laughed. "No, GarNell, the thing is, *he liked me.*"

"Oh."

"What ails you, GarNell? Why are you suddenly so interested in my love life? Did you think your poor old granny was likely to have become an old maid?"

That hushed me up. I felt her staring at me in the dark, and it made me uncomfortable.

"Since you're so curious, he had some relatives in Glenville and he was buried up there. That is worth mentioning in view of what happened after."

She stopped talking so I had to ask. "What happened?"

"Well, we had an awful flood that washed away a bunch of counties here, and it washed away the graveyard where Jason was buried."

"What do you mean washed away?"

"About twelve of them coffins up in the Glenville churchyard came down the Tuckasegee. There are folks that still talk about it. There are old guys on that liars bench down at the post office that claim they saw them. They talk about standing on the bridge in Dillsboro and watching them coffins go bouncing and bobbing down the river."

That image stunned me.

"Why is your mouth hanging open, GarNell?"

"Did they get them back?"

"Well, a couple of 'em got hung up under a bridge in Bryson City, so they got them back and reburied them . . . but the rest went on to the Mississippi . . . or the Gulf of Mexico." My grandmother got up and brushed the hulls from her apron. "Now, I have got to go find my flannel sheets, GarNell, because it is going to be cold tonight."

"Momma, do you know anything else about Jason's coffin?"

"Well, there is one thing." My grandmother stared into the darkness. "A couple of months after the flood, I got a postcard."

"What do you mean *a postcard?*"

"To be perfectly honest, I wasn't even sure that it was addressed to me because that postcard was in bad shape. It had been run over by something and it was creased and torn, but in spite of it all, there was my name, misspelled, but it was Agnis Puett. And there was his name, dim, but I could make it out. I could read the 'J' and 'on' was there. And the message on the other side was readable: 'Wish you were here,' and then that fancy 'J' he used to sign his name."

My grandmother went in the house. I guess it was five minutes before I followed her. "Are you saying you got a postcard from *a dead man?*"

"Good Lord! No, GarNell, I am just saying that I got a postcard."

"Did you keep it?"

"Probably. It might be in the Bible or I might've put it in one of my Rhinehart novels for safekeeping."

"Can I see it?"

"Maybe. I'll look for it."

I AM SITTING ON THE PORCH NOW, thinking about that postcard. Was my grandmother perverse? I hear her in the house where she is putting her flannel sheets on the bed. I think I heard her snicker.

I am pretty sure that I did.

The Hanging of Bayless Henderson

Nimrod Jarrett was one of the largest landowners in western North Carolina. In addition, he farmed and traded ginseng (he was involved in the operation of a "sang factory" in Haywood

County), owned mica and talc mines, and served in the Macon County militia, rising to the rank of colonel. The Jarrett family resided in Aquone until their house caught fire in 1855. Jarrett's youngest daughter perished in the flames. After this, the family moved to the Apple Tree Farm in Nantahala. Manley Wade Wellman's account of Jarrett's murder in a marvelous book, *Dead and Gone*, notes that Bayless Henderson probably heard speculation about Jarrett's wealth as he lounged on the porch of several stores and had probably seen the colonel ride by on his way to Franklin.

According to Henderson's belated confession, he waylaid Jarrett near Apple Tree Farm on the morning of September 15, 1873. He exchanged greetings with the colonel as he passed and then shot Jarrett in the back of the head. Jarrett fell, dying instantly, and his frightened horse bolted into the woods, dashing any hopes that Henderson had of recovering Jarrett's saddlebags. Henderson managed to steal the colonel's watch and a few coins but was forced to flee when he heard another rider approaching. This rider was Jarrett's wife, Nancy Avaline Jarrett, who had told her impatient husband that morning to leave without her and that she would overtake him later (Avaline was ten years younger than Nimrod but crippled by rheumatoid arthritis). Now, discovering her husband's body in the road, Nancy resisted the natural impulse to dismount. Instead, she rode onward to a neighbor's house and asked for assistance.

Returning with several neighbors, the group carried out a search of the scene and, in the process, discovered that they had been joined by a stranger with wet trousers who said he had just waded the Nantahala River to investigate why the group had gathered. When Jarrett's neighbors became suspicious and asked to see the stranger's shoes, he replied that if they intended to compare his shoes with the prints around the dead man's body, he could prove he was not the culprit since his shoes did not have heels and the prints around the body had been made by shoes with heels. This ingenious explanation did not reduce the group's suspicions and he was immediately arrested. En route to Franklin, he identified himself as Bayless Henderson, an itinerant worker from Tennessee.

Henderson did little to prove his innocence. His answers became increasingly vague and contradictory. He failed to give any information about his birth, family, or residence that could be verified. However, despite his vague testimony, his request for a second trial was granted. Bayless claimed to have new evidence, which turned out to be the fact that he was accused of murdering Nimrod S. Jarrett and the name of the deceased was given as N. S. Jarrett in the court documents. An impatient judge found Bayless's reasoning to be unacceptable since the two names obviously referred to the same man. Since there was evidence that due to the growing anger of Jarrett's friends in Macon County, the accused would not receive a fair trial there, the trial was moved to Webster, then the Jackson County seat.

Shortly thereafter, Henderson managed to escape but proved to be remarkably inept at hiding himself and was quickly found hiding in a brush pile and returned to his jail cell in Webster. So it was that after a series of postponements, the condemned man found himself on the gallows on May 6, 1874. Now comes one of those whimsical—if not downright bizarre—events that occur repeatedly in this odd story.

On the morning of Henderson's execution, a colorful group of teachers and ministers appeared in Webster. The group's mission was to evaluate the merits of schools in the region by visiting them, attending classes, studying the texts, and evaluating the qualifications of the teachers. Their final report was published in regional newspapers. Having completed their evaluation of the school at Hicksville, the group was on its way to attend classes in Jackson County schools when they encountered a large group of people congregating in Webster. Learning that the gathering was prompted by an execution, the group took the event in stride and joined the crowd, which they estimated to be about 3,000. As a consequence, we have a detailed account of Bayless's final hours prepared by this group and submitted to the *Carolina Citizen* newspaper in Asheville.

The atmosphere in Webster was decidedly festive. People had come from Macon, Jackson, and Haywood Counties. Picnic baskets were everywhere, and groups of young people strolled about the village streets. The scaffold had been erected on the village green, directly in front of the jailhouse doors. At 1:00 p.m., almost two hours before the scheduled execution, Henderson was conducted to it by Sheriff Bumgarner and Deputy Sheriff Allman. Several ministers were present and led the throng in singing and prayer.

It was noted that the condemned man seemed to be enjoying the affair. Several times he stood and gave solemn speeches about his sinful life and warned the youth in attendance to avoid his example. He spoke at length about his dissipated past, describing his crimes in lurid detail. Most of these details, however, when investigated following his execution, proved to be false. "The man was not only illiterate, he was ignorant," said one of his interviewers. He was also a natural-born liar.

The execution concluded with Bayless thanking the audience for coming. He gave several heartfelt statements of appreciation to Bumgarner and Allman. When the time came for Bayless to "hang suspended between heaven and hell," the plunge through the trap door failed to break his neck, but "the rope was so deeply embedded in the flesh that respiration, circulation and sensation were cut off like a lightning stroke." The body did not struggle or contort, but "a trembling as from a chill passed over him, about two minutes after he dropped." A physician came forward and pronounced him dead.

AS A CHILD, I often heard a traditional tale around Thanksgiving and Christmas about how several erstwhile physicians living in and around Webster were rumored to have robbed poor Bayless Henderson's grave in order to acquire body parts that would prove valuable in studying the functions of various bones. The tale has it that they divided Bayless between them . . . a tibia here, an ulna there, and so on. So it seems that finally Bayless rendered a valuable service to his fellow man.

There are a number of other stories . . . but I am sure they are all probably false. Perhaps they are best described as folklore. For example, my grandmother once told me that she and a group of teenage friends attended the hanging for the sole purpose of fainting. At the moment that Bayless fell through the trap door, they all fell backward from a fence. They all wore several elaborate petticoats that made a colorful display when they fell, like large flowers blooming.

My grandmother said their fall was a great success.

Blow the Tannery Whistle!

When I was a child, I awoke each morning to the mournful wail of our tannery whistle. It was a long wooooooooo that lingered in the coves and hollers of Jackson County for several moments. I would hear my grandmother's feet hit the floor and shortly afterward, the kitchen would be filled with the sounds and smells of breakfast.

The whistle was our clock, and it regulated our lives throughout the day. When it blew at noon, my grandmother would drop her hoe out in the garden and come in to put our dinner on the table. My grandfather, who drove an Esso truck, would hear the summons in Cullowhee or Barker's Creek, and he would come home to find his dinner ready for him. At 7:00 each evening, he would walk home, often passing members of the tannery's nightshift on their way to work.

Over the years, the town of Sylva became accustomed to waking, working, eating, and sleeping in accordance to the dictates of our tannery. We didn't all work there, but we moved in harmony to its tune.

There is an old story that the mayor of Sylva petitioned the tannery's manager to blow the whistle to celebrate civic events like football games, July 4th celebrations, and New Year's Day.

The manager steadfastly refused, sensibly observing that if the whistle blew at unspecified times, the workers would not know if they should come to work or go home. The mayor persisted. Finally, the manager agreed to blow the whistle, provided that some "noteworthy event" had occurred. He was the sole judge of the event's significance, of course. There weren't many noteworthy events.

The whistle blew for December 7, 1941. It blew again on V-J Day; and, finally, to everyone's embarrassment, it blew one October evening in 1947 to announce the "End of the World." (In actual fact, there was an aurora borealis, a northern lights display that badly frightened the people of western North Carolina.) The tannery manager, convinced that the Judgment Day was at hand, told the workers to go home "to be with their loved ones at this dread hour," and he blew the whistle. WOOOOOOOOO...

No one seems to remember this event. Perhaps it was embarrassing to admit that we had all been hoodwinked by an eerie spectacle that had been nothing more that the reflection of light from the polar caps. Regardless, it gave rise to an expression that is unique to Jackson County—an expression that only makes sense if you live here, or if you know the history of our whistle. The expression "blow the tannery whistle" became a means of (a) expressing amazement or astonishment and (b) acknowledging significance that is both rare and remarkable. In other words, something that would justify blowing our tannery whistle.

I remember my grandfather saying, "Blow the tannery whistle!" when his old-maid sister married an eighteen-year-old boy. My neighbors said it when my worthless uncle Ardell vanished and then returned several years later driving a Cadillac. My uncle Albert said it when I tied myself up, locked myself in our outhouse, and burned it down (I was attempting to simulate Gene Autry's escape from a burning miner's shack in a Saturday western). It was an expression that was always uttered with reverence and awe.

AFTER THE INCIDENT with the outhouse, I tried to avoid my grandfather and spent a lot of time with Charlie K. We hung out in Velt's Café and began to show up with a handful of quarters which we plugged into the big jukebox. I remember that Charlie's favorite song was a thunderous piano version of a classical piece, and Charlie would play it over and over. I guess we were thirteen or fourteen years old and just beginning to talk about girls. I think it was "Blue Tango" by Leroy Anderson.

One night, Charlie had a pocket full of quarters, and he would play "Blue Tango" six times for a quarter. I noticed that the waiters and the cook had all come out and they were staring at Charlie, who was doing a tango in front of the jukebox, and I got the feeling that everybody in Velt's was upset. Charlie had played the "Blue Tango" over fifteen times, and I think that was maybe ten times too many. We both had on our Teen Club clothes, and Charlie had his monogramed tie, blue with a red K for Kilpatrick, and I had my Valentino shirt . . . And when the song finally ended, Charlie plugged in another quarter and that is when Velt Wilson screamed "NO," and he came and unplugged the jukebox and pushed it down the hall into the kitchen. Velt suggested that Charlie and I should leave, and we did. I suggested that we take in the western at the Ritz, and so we did that . . . except there was no western at the Ritz. There was a Tarzan movie. I think it was *Tarzan's New York Adventure*.

I wasn't optimistic because I thought that since it was Saturday, the Ritz was honor bound to do a Lash LaRue, or a Roy Rogers . . . but, no! They were doing a Tarzan movie with Johnny Weissmuller! Well, I have to admit that Tarzan changed my life. I couldn't wait to get home and add Tarzan to my list of new friends. For the next couple of months, the Ritz ran a series of Tarzan movies, so I got acquainted with Boy and Cheetah and . . . *Jane*. I worked hard on Tarzan's yell and practiced it in the barn loft. In a short time, I had a regular routine in which I swung on a cow rope that I borrowed from the barn, and I got used to Cheetah going everywhere with me, and in time I rescued Cheetah when he fell into the Amazon River and was attacked by crocodiles. I had trouble getting along with Boy and tended to forget him, and although I always talked to Jane, her in her skimpy clothes, I didn't really understand why she was there.

But I had fun most of the time, until one afternoon, as Cheetah and I were swinging through the June apple tree in the front yard, when Cheetah fell into the river. Well I had to save that monkey, so I gave my Tarzan yell—it was kind of a yodel—and grabbed my imaginary knife and jumped into the Amazon. Well, the cow rope was tied around my waist and I didn't have enough rope to reach the ground. So, the rope stopped my fall and the jerk brought out a lot of June apples, and I was left hanging there, winding up in one direction, and then I would unwind in the opposite direction, and that rope was squeezing me in two, and I could only squeak, "Help." Pitiful. I was there for a long time, but finally one of our neighbors, Engle Woods, came down the trail with his lunchbox on his way to the tannery . . . and he heard that pitiful little squeak. I guess it was a month after that, that he told me that he thought I was dead. I wasn't, and he cut the rope and carried me to the porch and then he knocked on the door and when my grandfather came out, he said, "Arthur, thet young'en hanged hisself out there in thet June apple tree."

My grandfather told Engle that he was wore out trying to keep up with me and he mentioned my "bad blood." Well, it wasn't a week after that, he talked to Mr. Gibson, the county agent, who told my grandfather, "There isn't much wrong with GarNell. If you go to thet college at Cullowhee, there are a lot of kids thet act just like him."

TO MAKE A LONG STORY SHORT, my grandpa eventually did take me to WCTC and my high school principal, Henry Galloway, got me a vocational scholarship because I had had polio. I ended up staying in a dorm and only came home to get my laundry done. Well, what can I say? I was delighted to be in a place where there were others that were a lot like me. I joined the drama club, wrote for the college newspaper, and sat up all night with others, drinking coffee and talking about the meaning of life. When I actually made it to graduation, I came home to find my grandfather in bad shape. He sat at the end of the porch with the big family Bible in his lap. My grandmother told me that she would tell him about my approaching graduation.

The day I graduated, I was standing in front of Hoey Auditorium when I spotted my grandfather in his old pickup truck. He parked at the Townhouse, and my uncle Asbury said, "I will have to go get him. He's weak, but I'll walk him back." He did that. When my grandfather was standing in front of me, he was breathing hard, but when he could finally speak, he said, "Well, blow the tannery whistle."

THE WHISTLE IS GONE, of course, as are most of the people who used to rise, eat, work, and sleep when it called them. Sometimes, I wake in the night thinking I hear that mournful wooooooooooo echoing through my holler. For a moment, I am back in a world filled with laughter, childish innocence, and possibility.

Tiny

I have been thinking about this little woman a great deal lately. Her name was Tinnie Tolley Cagle and she died on May 9, 1984. I think that her first name is actually a misspelling of her nickname, "Tiny." Since she was born on July 14, 1897, and died on May 3, 1984, we know she lived to be eighty-six. Other details of her life are uncertain. Her birth certificate gives Clay County as her birthplace but she once told me that she thought she was born in Georgia. Maybe not—she was never sure. Her husband Robinson Cagle's death certificate notes that he was married to "Ina" Cagle. An accompanying document lists his wife as "Ida" Cagle. The misinformation seems endless.

Tiny and her husband Robinson were my neighbors for two decades, and I have vague memories of them forty years before that when I frequently saw them sitting on a bench below the old Welch & Cable store. They were lively, waving at people passing and calling out to friends. They attracted attention because they were oddly mismatched. Robinson was tall and lank, while Tiny was not much more than four feet tall, due to her malformed spine. When standing, Tiny looked like a question mark. She was sensitive about her appearance and always attempted to face people, trying to avoid turning her back. When I knew her well enough to ask, I once inquired about the deformity. "A mean ole boy hit me with a rake," she said. "I was just a baby." Then, she smiled, which is something she did a lot. "Sit down 'n I'll git you a Coca Coly."

The little shack where Tiny and Robinson lived was located in a bend of the Cherry Street road that was thick in rhododendron and laurel. In midsummer, the foliage sometimes concealed part of the house and a passing motorist might only catch glimpses of Tiny and Robinson's smiling faces peering out at them. People who walked by were often greeted by Tiny, who would often come into the road to talk to people, inviting them to "come and sit on the porch." I think it was then that I would often feel that this odd couple was not of this earth. It was as though they originated in a fairyland filled with magical creatures, and that perhaps they had ventured through a magic door into our harsh world of speeding cars and barking dogs. The door had closed and they were unable to return, so they were condemned to stay here, dependent on the uncertain charity of our world.

When I became a frequent visitor, I was sometimes invited inside, where I found an astonishing collection of cast-off items. Three-legged chairs, odd pieces of linoleum on a wooden floor, lots of religious pictures, a small wood stove, a ramshackle bed, and an ancient sink. I don't think there was an "icebox." There was no hot water or indoor plumbing, but

Tiny had a remarkable water system. It ran through a rubber tube from a neighbor's spring, under the road and into Tiny's kitchen, running continually.

IN THE SUMMER when the neighbor's gardens were in full production, I would sometimes see baskets of tomatoes, beans, and okra. I remember once, she came into the road and stopped my car, clapping her little hands, "Honey, I have a peck of peaches. Come have one." If you didn't stop her, she would load a cracked plate with a mix of cream corn, a can of Vienna sausage, a Moon Pie, and Ritz crackers. When I drove by in mid-December and saw smoke from the chimney, I wondered what they were living on. It pained me to think of the two, huddled in that house, feeding wood to that little stove. Any inquiry was dismissed with a great, beaming smile. "Oh, Honey, we are fine. Had eggs and a biscuit for breakfast." Did they? I hope so.

Tiny had a habit that sometimes brought the local police to her house. She stood in the middle of that snug little curve that went around her house while she played sentinel. The place where she stood was called Tiny's Curve. (The name had a certain irony since it also described this little woman's spine.) Usually, after a near mishap in which a vehicle swerved into the ditch to avoid hitting her, the police would explain why she couldn't stand in the road like that. Tiny would smile and nod. She would ask the policeman his name and ask if he liked cats. That was the real problem. Tiny's cats.

Early each morning, they would come boiling out from under that little shack, a great multitude of orange, gray, and black, and Tiny would feed them. She had condensed milk and sacks of pellets, scraps of bread and meat. I think she must have spent the majority of every day gathering that feast. She sat on a little stool and held court, chanting a strange little nonsense song. She talked to those cats and each one had a name: Queenie, Rose, Billy, Mary, Linda Lou, Patches, Blackie, Betty, Big Mouth, Sweetie, on and on. She inquired about their wounds and checked them for problems.

I GUESS YOU SEE what is coming. A week rarely passed without a fatality. I would drive by to see a mangled kitten in the road. Tiny removed them all and buried them behind the house. Then she would say harsh things about cars and dogs.

I remember a summer when I was sitting on their porch with Robinson and he was telling me about the time he was snakebit some forty years ago. He would remove his shoe and trace a crooked scar with his finger. "I was working for the WPA," he said, "clearing brush. Thought I was going to die. After that I couldn't work without fainting." It was in the midst of this tale that the car came. It was coming much too fast and there, as always, was Tiny in the middle of the road. The driver swerved and skidded. He ended up with his SUV in the yard, just a few feet from where Robinson and I sat. An entire family stared at us and we stared back. Meanwhile, Tiny was busy picking up gravel on the side of the road and when she had a good handful, she came and threw it at the SUV. Robinson stood and spoke to the driver. "I'm real sorry about that. She is crazy and I can't do a thing with her."

By that time, Tiny had returned with another handful of gravel, which she threw at the windshield. The driver made an attempt to back up and then decided to get out and talk to Tiny who had by then gathered another handful of gravel. The driver reconsidered and got back in his car and began to drive away, but Tiny got him through the open window with gravel, sand, and a cloud of dust.

After that, Tiny returned to her post, scouting Cherry Street for cars and dogs. Robinson went back to telling me about the hardships of working for the WPA and Tiny went back to reporting on the dangers of living on Cherry Street. "I see a red car with a Georgia tag down at Painters," she said. "Must be that daughter that lives in Atlanta, home for a visit." Tiny prowls the roadside, like some ancient mariner, searching the sea for threats, her hand shielding her eyes. Then, she announces alarm. "Old black dog, prowling around the Carden barn and . . . it is coming this way. Looks like a cat killer."

ALL OF THIS was twenty years ago. Time moved on as it must and one morning, as I was leaving for work, I found Tiny standing at the foot of my driveway. "I gotta go away," she said, "both me and Robinson. They putting me in the hospital and I guess we will end up in the county home." Tiny was crying a little, but she was smiling as always. "I was wondering, would you feed my cats?" She grabbed my hand through the window. "I'll pay you back." I said I would.

Tiny and Robinson ended up in a complex social services agency runaround that left them in different locations. Both were dead within two years. The machinery of progress swept up Cherry Street, taking the little shack on Tiny's Curve like chaff in the wind. Nothing remains now except a space devoid of habitation, cats, or interest.

OKAY FOLKS, I AM SORRY but I am going to get sentimental here and say something corny. If there is a Heaven, I sincerely hope that there is a little rhododendron thicket just inside, and that Tiny and Robinson are sitting there, in that fey little vine-covered shack, greeting the new arrivals. I would like to think that they finally got back into that magical land from whence they came long ago when they crossed the boundary between Heaven and Rhodes Cove. Of course, I also hope that there are no cars in sight and that there are lots of cats on the porch.

Christmas in Cowee

My Christmas Eve experience in 1952 begins in Dillsboro, where my grandfather stopped to get gas from Cap Weaver, who ran a little Esso station directly across the street from the Jarrett House. Cap stayed open early and late, and since he had a Bermuda Bell, it got him in trouble. It rang each time a customer stopped at his station. The Bermuda Bells give a loud

DING-DANG that can be heard a mile away, so when Cap's bell sounded around midnight, lights came on all over Dillsboro and angry phone calls were made.

Cap was an old bachelor who slept on a cot in the station with a couple of hounds. I liked him since he always came to the car with a Guess What?, which was a kind of candy that no longer exists (a kind of early Cracker Jack). Cap warned my grandfather that there was snow in Cowee and we might find ourselves stuck on the mountain. This was the old road, a looping, crooked trip which went along the river and then up the Cowee Mountain to Clark's Place where there was a big waterwheel.

Before we got to the top of the mountain, the snow was falling heavy, a slow snow that fell with deceptive gentleness. Before long, Grandpa had to stop occasionally and get out and prod the snow to be sure we were still on the concrete. After we passed Rickman's store, we were down to a crawl, but my grandfather was stubborn. He intended to spend Christmas with his mother.

WHEN WE TOOK THE LITTLE CUTOFF going to Aunt Nancy's (that is what everyone called my great-grandmother), we managed to cross the little bridge over the creek that ran by Aunt Nancy's house. He stopped and said we could walk from there. We got out and found the snow to be over knee-high and still falling. We walked slowly and I followed Grandpa, who knew where he was. Before we had gone 100 yards, we saw the house, and the porch was crowded with relatives. I recognized the barn and the springhouse. The outhouse was memorable, since it was over the creek, which was what was called a "bold stream." When we finally climbed the steps, we found ourselves surrounded by Daltons, Gibsons, and Hursts. We were ushered into the house where we were greeted by Aunt Nancy.

My great-grandmother, Aunt Nancy Hurst Carden, was in a bed that had a straight-backed chair in it with a pillow placed against the chair's back, propping her up. There she sat, in her nineties, erect and facing her visitors. Over the years, I discovered that this was not an uncommon scene. Poor folks in Appalachia often created this throne where the treasured grandmothers could greet company. Aunt Nancy had cataracts and was partially deaf, but she ruled her household and made most of the domestic decisions.

We were ushered to the fireplace, which was huge and contained two- and three-foot-long firelogs. As we stood in a puddle of melting snow, I noticed the writing on the wall above the fireplace. "God Bless This School." This was the room where children were taught, and Cardens were the teachers. Along one wall was an impressive shelf for books, which the local bookmobile kept stocked (I read my first Jesse Stewart novel here).

The meal that night was awesome, and most of it was brought by the relatives. We ate leather britches, creamed corn, tenderloin, and gritted cornbread. After supper, we all sat around Aunt Nancy's bed as she told stories . . . wonderful stories that featured bears, flash floods, and forest fires. Eventually, people began to take their leave. All of them lived nearby. Even so, I didn't envy them the trip home.

GRANDPA AND I SLEPT in the attic, so we climbed the rickety steps that were stacked with tintypes, all of them photographs that had been developed in the sun. Aunt Nancy's husband had been a photographer. She told me, "Jest about ever-body that lives in Cowee has their picture here." We slept in a feather bed and I had no trouble going to sleep, woke in the morning to find little rows of snow on my quilt . . . it had drifted in through the roof slats during the night. We came down to a big breakfast: ham and eggs and cat-head biscuits, red-eye gravy and sourwood honey. I was told to wash my hands before I ate and I found the water frozen in the wash pan.

It had finally stopped snowing and Grandpa was determined to go to the Cove, a piece of land that he owned, maybe thirty or forty acres. My grandfather talked about it often and said that he planned to move into that remote cove someday, and he hoped to never hear another car horn for the rest of his life. There were quail and partridge everywhere, and he would have chickens that "roosted in the trees." The Cove had several springs so he would have plenty of water.

Back at Aunt Nancy's, the neighbors were gathered around her bed as she told about the night of a winter storm, perhaps ten years ago, when someone knocked at the door near to midnight. Aunt Elsie opened the door to find three convicts who said, "We are freezing, ma'am." Great Granny invited them in and gave them a place in front of the fire, and Cousin Irene took them to the barn and gave them blankets and quilts. They ate their breakfast the following morning and washed the plates in the snow . . . and then they were gone. One of them returned several years later with his wife and infant son. "You saved us," he said. She still got Christmas cards from him.

THAT IS ALL BURIED in the past now. After Aunt Nancy died, the house burned and all of those Hursts and Daltons scattered to the four winds. My grandfather found himself paying medical bills for ailing relatives, and so he sold the Cove. It is full of condominiums now, and the quail and partridge have vanished. My grandfather is buried in Love's Field near the highway. I hope he does not hear the traffic.

The Rhodes Cove Grinch

Being a diabetic with hearing problems (especially in crowds), I have days when I probably shouldn't be "out and about." A few months ago, when I was attempting to read the menu in a local restaurant without my glasses, I noticed that the decibel level resembled Walmart on Christmas Eve. The lights were too bright, the TVs (several of them) were proclaiming world disasters, and a child was screaming in the next booth. I guess I ended up staring about in confusion. Then, the waitress smiled and said, "And what does Mr. Grumpy want this morning."

Mr. Grumpy? Was she talking to me? Then, I caught my reflection in a mirror above the counter and saw that I looked a bit like the old Irish actor Barry Fitzgerald—a crusty old geezer who always looked like he was sucking a lemon as he threatened folks with his walking stick and said things like, "Ahh, you dirty git."

Now, here is the thing. I wasn't feeling especially contentious. In fact, this was one of my better days. The problem was, my facial expression was at odds with my disposition. When I told a friend about the comment by the waitress, his response surprised me. He said that I had a reputation as being a bit . . . crusty.

"Crusty?"

"Yeah, you know, a bit of a curmudgeon."

"Really? Well, thank you for brightening my day."

"There now, see what I mean?"

OKAY, SO I AM A BIT TESTY. Aside from the fact that I think a lot of this has to do with ill-fitting dentures, I'm not sure that I am ready to let my acquaintances provide me with a label. I mean, isn't that a kind of self-fulfilling prophecy? Since I have become aware that I am Mr. Grumpy, I feel an obligation to act like the person I am perceived to be. Now, when people don't agree with my taste in literature, movies, and politics, I realize that I have an opportunity to be downright abusive without actually offending anyone. They merely look at each other and smile because they have "pulled my chain," and I have lapsed into my role as a contentious old geezer: the Rhodes Cove Grinch.

So, the fact that I usually have a frustrated expression on my face . . . well, this facade does not honestly reflect my inner self—my *complacent, gentle soul,* you understand. Now . . . it *is* true that I am occasionally disgruntled by some computer problems (AOL is a blundering, incompetent and arrogant entity, and I have told them so frequently), and come to think of it, I was a bit outspoken when Duke Power doubled my electrical bill. Well, all this rancor developed about the same time that the company contracted to pave the street in front of my house cut down over twenty trees on my property without consulting me and I began proclaiming my discontent to the neighborhood. But, usually, such events are just minor blemishes on my otherwise sunny disposition. Really.

Recently, I have been eating lunch in the Jackson County Senior Citizen Center, and I think I have stumbled into a brotherhood there. The other day, an old coot set his tray down at my table and stared at me.

"Aren't you the jolly soul," he said.

"There are plenty of empty tables in here. Why don't you move?"

"Well, to tell you the truth," he said, "I feel it is my civic duty to run you out of here so the rest of us can eat without looking at your face."

"Lots of luck," I said. "Who the hell are you anyway?"

"Don't recognize me, huh? I'm one of your old neighbors from Rhodes Cove. If I remember correctly, you shot me with your Daisy air rifle once."

"Good for me," I said. After more of this camaraderie, I finished my lunch and got up to leave.

"See you tomorrow," he said.

"Not likely," I said. "You dirty git."

FRANKLY, I'M LOOKING FORWARD to tomorrow's lunch. Chicken and dumplings with a kindred soul.

The *Lucky Strike Hit Parade*

When I was twelve years old, I developed into a strange young'en. I waited every evening until my grandparents went to the barn to perform the nightly ritual of milking the cow, feeding all of the animals and shutting them into their prisons . . . the chickens here, the cow in her stall, the pig in his pen, and so on. All of this took over one hour.

During that time, I was alone in the old farmhouse and—unknown to my grandparents—I morphed into a multitalented performer. I turned on the *Lucky Strike Hit Parade* on the big Silvertone radio in the living room, and I accompanied the program as folks like Vaughn Monroe, Tennessee Ernie Ford, Doris Day, Frankie Lane, and Guy Lombardo devoted their talents to paying tribute to the musical "hits." I accompanied each performer, and sometimes I responded to their requests to assist . . . perhaps to harmonize with Nat King Cole in his current chart-topper. I modestly agreed, much as his daughter would do in a future generation. My adolescent, high tenor voice would harmonize with Tex Williams or Perry Como and—if the occasion called for it—I would fetch my grandfather's fiddle and mime to a popular version of the melodramatic tune "Temptation," complete with a nasal hillbilly squeal. The *Lucky Strike Hit Parade* lasted for the better part of an hour, and if I sometimes saw my grandparents making an early return with a bucket of milk, I would hide all of my props and collapse in a chair, pretending to read a comic book. I would often hear my grandparents discuss me in the kitchen. "What is he doing?" and the response, "Reading. That is all he ever does."

"Ho, ho," I would chuckle. "Little do you know what wild, raging talents boil within this youthful breast."

THOSE WERE STRANGE YEARS for music in America. Some of the worst music ever written came out of the period immediately following World War II. There was an abundance of silly, funny songs like "Lavender Blue, Dilly, Dilly" or the one that went "Abadabadaba, said the monkey to the chimp." Amazingly, they all made it to the *Hit Parade*, and although their stay may have been brief, I memorized and loved each and every one. For years, my favorite was a smiling, chain-smoking fellow named Phil Harris, who sang my favorite song:

> I know a place called Do Wah Ditty
> It ain't no town, it ain't no city
> It's awfully small, but it's awfully pretty!
> And that is what I like about the South

He had another favorite tune that went,

> Tell Saint Peter at the golden gate
> That you hate to make him wait
> But I just gotta have another cigarette

He ended up on the *Jack Benny Show* and, of course, cigarettes finally killed him.

But all I really wanted to tell you about was that silly little kid that raced around the house miming lyrics to his favorite songs while keeping a watchful eye out for his grandparents. For that brief hour each night, he was a multitalented genius who was the adored performer for millions. Did other kids do that? I think not. It didn't carry over into my school performances either. I was a mediocre to poor student with few friends . . . except for the equally strange kid, Charlie K. I kept pace as a homely little kid from Rhodes Cove with a stash of forbidden comic books hidden in the feed room at Ensley's store, where I hid on summer afternoons with an RC Cola and a dangerously uncontrolled imagination. My uncle Albert discovered my secret passion for bad music and would sometimes take me with him to Maple Springs, where he would prompt me to sing for the girls who adored Uncle Albert, and I would stand in the middle of a dark room where people where dancing and whispering, and I would sing:

> In the sleepy town of San Juanita,
> There's a story that the padre tells
> of a gay señor and señorita,
> And the serenade of the bells.

Sometimes, they would buy me an RC and a Baby Ruth.

Dr. Blosser's Cigarettes

By the time I was six, I had discovered that the house where I lived with my grandparents was filled with secrets and mystery. It did me little good to ask my grandparents for answers, for they would look at each other and silently shake their heads. So I had to do my own research. I became a spy! I discovered that if I crawled through the dark kitchen around midnight and placed my nose in the space between my grandparents' bedroom door and the floor, I sometimes heard the answer to one of my questions. I learned that my mother was in a place called Knoxville, and that she was married again.

    Sometimes, when my grandparents were working in the garden, I would sneak into their bedroom and open the big chest of drawers that sat in the corner. The bottom drawer slid out to reveal my grandmother's hot water bottle, and nestled next to it, there was a big, black pistol. It was very heavy, and I had to use both hands when I lifted it. I always aimed it at the picture on the wall of two kids crossing a little bridge during a storm. They were accompanied by an angel. I was always careful to place the pistol back in the same position. I knew that a pistol had killed my father and made me an orphan. I sometimes sat for several minutes staring at that weapon. I sometimes brought a playmate, and we sat together and passed the pistol back and forth.

    If I crept through the garden in the evening, and if I sneaked up the steps to the barn loft, I could lay in the hay and listen to my grandparents milk the cow. Sometimes, they talked about me; they said that I was "quare," and they worried that I might have "bad blood" from my mother's side of the family. They sometimes discussed the possibility of taking me to Knoxville.

THERE WAS ANOTHER chest of drawers in the dining room, and the top drawer was where my grandfather kept all the unguents and cures that he ordered from Dr. John R. Brinkley on XERA, the "sunshine station between the nations." There were "Crazy Water Crystals," which were a laxative; Hadacol, which soothed an upset stomach; Colorback, which "renewed" gray hair; Black Draught, which my grandfather called a "spring tonic" (it was also a laxative). Now we come to my favorite, "Dr. Blosser's Cigarettes." This was a "medical cigarette" which treated catarrh and asthma, and it came in a big, red box. I had been planning to smoke a Dr. Blosser for a long time. I finally took two and retired to the barn.

Dr. Blosser's Cigarettes are a nauseous and vile experience. I discovered that there was something that looked like a cough drop in the center of the cig, and the message on the box assured me that, instead of tobacco, Dr. Blosser used a mix of exotic herbs. My eyes watered and I gagged a few times, but I stuck it out. You see, I really wanted to smoke! I had watched my favorite actors smoke with abandon, snorting smoke through their nostrils and handling a cigarette in a manner that made them appear graceful and poised.

I told my best friend, Charlie K., about Dr. Blosser's Cigarettes, and he was immediately agreeable: we should learn to smoke like pros, and we should conduct an experiment in front of the ticket booth at the Ritz Theater . . . on Saturday. We showed up at the Ritz on the following Saturday. I guess we were eight or nine years old. Don "Red" Berry was starring in *The Dalton Gang*. I went first, lighting my cigarette with one of my grandmother's kitchen matches. I had a bunch of adults staring at me, but I was prepared. I gave them a James Cagney sneer and snorted some smoke through my nose. Then I lighted Charlie's cigarette. We had rehearsed this part, and we sneered and snorted smoke in unison. Finally, we flipped our cigs to the sidewalk and ground them out with our shoe heels. Then we strolled on into the Ritz. Of course, after a moment, we returned and picked up our mashed cigs; they might be good for another performance!

I don't know how long it would have gone on had we not found reason to stop. But there came a Saturday when I blew smoke at the wrong person. It was my uncle Albert, who was a big fan of Saturday westerns. Snatching the Dr. Blosser from my mouth, he said, "What the hell do you think you are doing, kid?"

I explained that we were "just smoking."

He stared at the Dr. Blosser and he said, "Where did you get this thing?" I told him about the Dr. Blosser, and he finally laughed. "You got Daddy's medical cigarettes!" But he stopped laughing and said, "Let me tell you what is going to happen now!" He took our cigarettes and tore them apart and scattered them around us. "No more of this, kid. You and your sidekick can go on inside and see Lash LaRue in *The Return of the Lash*." We did that.

BY THE TIME I was a senior in high school, I was a seasoned smoker. I tried to mimic James Dean and Marlon Brando. When I went to Atlanta for a year, I got a job in a trucking line called Flanagan, the Moving Man, and I sat all day in a tiny room with a huge ash tray and three telephones that rang constantly. My job was to direct drivers to other jobs. It was tension-ridden and I quickly got to smoking four packs a day. When I returned to Sylva, I had a bad cough, and an X-ray revealed that I had a spot on one lung. When Doctor Morgan showed me the spot on my lung, he suddenly reached across his desk and snatched the Raleighs from my shirt pocket and tore them into little pieces. After he dumped them in the wastebasket, he said, "Go buy yourself another pack! If you keep smoking, you will be on one of those little oxygen tanks that you have to take with you everywhere you go. I will wager that you will be dead within three years."

Dr. Morgan scared me. My uncle Albert, who was a chain-smoker, already had one of those little wheeled tanks that he dragged behind him when he came home for a visit. So, I quit, but it was the hardest thing I ever did. Since I was a seasoned, four-pack smoker, I had a difficult withdrawal. I had huge blue bruises all over me, which Dr. Morgan said were caused by nicotine withdrawal. I had a lot of problems. I ground my teeth in my sleep and lost all of my teeth. I developed a short temper, which got me in a lot of trouble. It took six months before I stopped craving cigarettes. I still smoke in my dreams.

The Kingdom of the Happy Land

Sometime before the end of the Civil War, when "Father Abraham" had abolished slavery, thousands of African Americans found themselves facing an uncertain future. They were called "freedmen," but how would they live? Where would they go? Many moved aimlessly through the ravaged South like nomads, living off the land, searching for direction and community. The very earth seemed hostile.

In this desperate time, a number of men appeared who said, "Follow me." One such man was a slave named William. According to a nearly forgotten tale, he had once lived on a great plantation in Mississippi. However, he had been blessed by fortune. His father was a white man, which had provided his son with some advantages. William became a house servant and was taught to read and write. Blessed with a quick mind and a profound intellect, he became a leader at an early age, serving as a preacher and adviser to his people. He eventually married a slave named Luella. When freedom came, William, who had adopted the name of his former owner and father, Montgomery, called his freed brethren together and told them of his plan.

According to the story that has been passed down, William had heard of a land to the east. It was located at the foot of a mountain and encircled by a river. It could be reached by a great highway over which ceaseless multitudes passed—droves of cattle, wagons laden with meat and molasses, merchants, drivers, and stagecoaches—moving back and forth between the low country and the mountains. William Montgomery told his people that their promised land lay in the valleys and coves of those mountains. "There, we can own land, till the soil and raise a family," he said. "If we stay together and help each other, we will prosper. Remember, all for one and one for all."

Approximately 150 freedmen cast their lot with Montgomery and departed Mississippi for a new beginning in the east. The ravaged land through which they passed provided meager sustenance. The ruined fields sometimes yielded chickpeas, potatoes, and yams. As they moved across Alabama and into South Carolina, they sometimes caught half-wild mules and horses—animals that would be useful in the promised land. They often passed nights camped near streams and found shelter for themselves and their animals beneath trees or in abandoned barns. Everywhere they encountered other freedmen, and as their little caravan progressed, their numbers grew.

In the stories passed down about the "first comers," when Montgomery and his followers entered South Carolina and found the fabled road that passed through places named Enoree River, Callahan Mountain, and Winding Stair, they began hearing stories that verified the existence of their promised land, a place in the mountains to which the white folks made annual pilgrimages, somewhere up in the high country where tracts of uninhabited land stretched for miles.

At the North Carolina line, shortly after they had passed the wreckage of Union breastworks that had once blocked all travel on the road, they came to a place called Oakland, the home of Col. John Davis and his wife, "Miss Serepta." The property was located near the present town of Tuxedo, in Henderson County.

Some of the freedmen Montgomery encountered in the area told him that the widowed Miss Serepta and her son Tom owned thousands of acres of farmland, now idle and unplowed.

Miss Serepta's former slaves were gone to seek their fortune elsewhere, and all of Colonel Davis's livestock and possessions had been swept away by marauders and the Union troops. The aging lady and her son Tom, now virtually penniless, were struggling to survive by providing food and lodging for the few random travelers, journeymen who were beginning to appear again on the great road, en route to North Carolina and Tennessee. For William Montgomery and his band, Oakland proved an opportunity heaven-sent.

Miss Serepta readily agreed to William's offer: shelter and food in exchange for domestic chores. As winter turned to spring, the "first comers" began plowing, planting, and repairing Oakland's old slave quarters. The few animals that had survived the long journey were kept in a dilapidated barn. The mountainside yielded firewood and timber for log houses—each with a chimney constructed from chunks of granite dug from the surrounding hillsides. The Happy Land had begun.

There is no way of knowing the original population of the Happy Land, but it is likely that their numbers grew as word spread of the settlement on the Carolina border. Over time, William and his followers assisted Miss Serepta and her son in converting Oakland into a thriving lodging house, a place where travelers and visitors could stay throughout the summer and into the fall. The first comers tended the gardens, raised the broilers and fryers, milked the cows, churned the butter, and did the laundry. Oakland flourished and eventually William approached his landlady with a request to buy tracts of land at one dollar an acre. Miss Serepta agreed.

Weary freedmen continued to arrive for years. A group came from Coe Ridge, Kentucky; others came from devastated plantations in Georgia and lower South Carolina. There is evidence that suggests that by 1870, the total population of the Kingdom exceeded 400.

According to the descendants of the original settlers, Montgomery developed a communal settlement with himself and his wife Luella as king and queen. Almost a century later, descendants of the original settlers would recall that their parents and grandparents had spoken vaguely of William's desire to recreate an African tribal village, complete with ancient rituals and customs. William and Luella had adjoining cabins, which contained thrones. Further, legend asserts that the "royal cabins" were constructed on the boundary between North Carolina and South Carolina with William's cabin in North Carolina and Luella's in South Carolina—a precaution that was designed to save half of the Kingdom should unforeseen events cause the loss of the other.

As both Oakland and Montgomery's Kingdom prospered, William's followers sought employment as craftsmen and laborers throughout the region. Often working for as little as ten cents a day, the first comers gave their earnings to William, who always accepted the money restating his old admonishment, "All for one and one for all." Montgomery deposited the funds in a common treasury. In time King William began dispensing money at his discretion. He established communal gardens, developed a network of storage barns, and bought more land. By 1873, the Kingdom of the Happy Land had become an independent, self-sustaining community.

As commerce thrived throughout the region, Happy Land developed a diversity of trades and crafts. Taking advantage of the great road that had brought them to Oakland, the Happy Landers became teamsters, sending wagons loaded with produce to the surrounding towns and cities. Carpenters, weavers, and basket makers thrived, and with the approval of the king and queen, the skilled craftsmen sometimes sought employment and lodging in nearby places. However, they returned at intervals to the Kingdom with their earnings, committed to the dream of owning their own land, a communal tract where married couples could build a cabin and raise a family.

One of the old tales concerns a popular product called Happy Land Liniment, a concoction of herbs and unguents that was provided by the king and queen to their followers for the treatment of rheumatism and aching muscles. Other potions with curative powers were also available, including a Balm in Gilead that was made from catnip, which purportedly improved appetite and general well-being.

In time, the original founders of the Kingdom, including William Montgomery, died, and subsequently many of the details of the Kingdom's origin and history were lost. One of several conflicting stories notes that William had made careful plans for his succession, and that his brother Robert had been prepared to take his place. One of the details that has survived regarding King William's death is a fragmented account of a Happy Land ceremony in which the mournful chant "the king is dead" is replaced by a triumphant "long live the king" as the new ruler took his place in the vacant throne chair.

After the Kingdom broke up about 1900, former residents moved to nearby towns, where they acquired employment as tradesmen and servants. In later years they told stories and anecdotes about their lives in "an earthly Eden." They remembered an old granite stepping stone that marked the site of a chapel in which children were trained and weekly religious services were conducted. Oral tradition in the region recalls the "Kingdom Singers," organized by Queen Luella, which traveled every summer throughout the settlement and beyond, performing musical programs.

One of the most interesting tales deals with a Black, itinerate minister, Reverend Ezel, who appears to have been a self-appointed recruiter for the Kingdom. Preaching in small towns throughout South Carolina, Ezel acquired many followers in the vicinity of Newbury, Union, Cross Anchor, and Enoree, where he sometimes assumed the role of a nineteenth-century Moses who led the chosen to the Happy Land. Apparently, Reverend Ezel did not become a resident himself but continued to preach in remote townships. In 1957, an eighty-five-year-old resident of Hendersonville, Ezel Couch, vowed that he was born in 1872 and was named for a traveling minister. Couch stated that his family lived in Union, South Carolina, and he was brought to the Kingdom by his parents when he was one year old.

TODAY, ONLY FOLK TALES and a handful of anecdotes note the existence of the once thriving settlement. With the coming of the railroad, the region discovered a more efficient means of transporting wares and produce. The great road, which had brought Montgomery's band to Oakland and provided their community access to markets, fell into disuse. Happy Land's wagons, the lifeblood of the Kingdom, became obsolete. By 1900, virtually all of the residents had departed, and within a decade most of the original structures had fallen. Today, visitors find nothing but a few chimneys and the collapsed gravestones in the cemetery—none of which retain the names of the deceased.

In 1910, a portion of the land where the Kingdom had once thrived (now called Stanton Mountain, near Greenville, South Carolina) was bought by a local farmer, Joe Bell. In time, he dismantled and removed the original homes. In 1985, Joe's grandson Ed and his uncle Frank agreed to be interviewed about their memories of the Kingdom and made a return trip to the original site with a group of students from Northwest Middle School in Traveler's Rest, South Carolina.

Standing in the rubble of a cabin, the two men pointed to the location of William and Luella Montgomery's cabins, the remains of a graveyard, and what may have once been the location of a schoolhouse and a chapel. Nothing remained except a shattered chimney and a wilderness of lush undergrowth. When asked, "What was here in 1900?" Frank Bell said, "I remember standing on this hill." He then pointed to the wilderness before him and said, "As far as I could see down that valley, there were corncribs—hundreds and hundreds of corncribs."

Love's Field

Kind hearts, I think I have mentioned that I have serious insomnia. I often stare at the ceiling for the better part of eight to ten hours in a state that is neither waking nor sleeping but some status that is neither. I did it again last night and found myself standing in Love's Field where my grandparents are buried, yet I was also aware that my cat Prissy was asleep under my left hand and I felt her warmth and purr and the rise and fall of her body. I knew that I could make the whole setting vanish by simply rising from my bed and sending Prissy off to the kitchen to check out her food dish, but I kept the peace and stared at the old, white Methodist church (which is no longer there) and I walked to my grandfather's grave.

I wasn't surprised to find him sitting on the little grassy plot, staring at the traffic on 107, and I remember that he had always hated the sound of traffic, and of course, he is aware of the irony of the fact that the traffic has increased and there is a new highway that is designed to come through that will make the noise unimaginable, a mix of sounds like an ocean surf, and I remember the sound of his voice as we drove up Glenville Mountain with a caravan of frustrated drivers behind us, blowing their horns to no avail for we are going ten miles per hour with over a thousand gallons of gasoline for Howard Zachary, and there are no pullovers on Glenville Mountain (although they are there now) and my grandfather looks at me and begins his litany that I have heard a hundred times about his retirement and that cove in Macon County that he will move to and there is no sound of traffic there, just peace and wind and running water, but wait! We are not on Glenville Mountain; no, we are simply pretending to be in Love's Field in two conflicting times—before and after the old Methodist church—and I am neither here nor there, but sitting beside my grandfather by his grave and I am speaking.

I say, "Hello, Grandpa," and his head turns, and he looks at me in what I can only call alarm, for he never quite knew what to think of me, but he finally smiles and he says, "Well, Lo and Behold! It's the quare young'en, all grown up and aged. I hear you have made a name for yore self. Telling stories! Is that it?" He stares away across the graveyard and up at the abiding mountains. "I never knowed what to think about you, GarNell. I allus had serious doubts about yore sanity. Actually thought you were sorta like my brother Frank that ended up in thet mental health hospital in Morganton. I was disappointed that you never learned to play a musical instrument. Agnes allus said that you were . . . what was the word? 'Peverse.' Something that you got from yore mother."

He grows quiet then, and we sit for a while . . . I am sitting by a man that I loved dearly, but never knew how to tell him that, and of all of the heartbreak both he and I had known, the one that had pained me most was the fact that he saw nothing of merit in me. Finally, I say, "I know a great deal about you, Grandpa. I know about Buddy, your son that was never acknowledged. He came to see me."

"Stop right there! I don't want to talk about that. I never knew what you might become. You became a teacher, and a writer, and *a storyteller* . . . maybe that is why I am a little afraid of you, GarNell. You have got no call to talk about that. You need to hush."

Suddenly, he is gone and so is Love's Field, the church, and the tombstones, and here I am alone staring at the ceiling, and Prissy moves beneath my hand and purrs.

Outside, Looking In

The first time I became aware of what it meant to be "outside looking in," I was nine years old. It was a cold, snowy day in December and my cat Bobbie was asleep in front of the fireplace. I was reading my favorite funny book about Submariner when my grandfather came in from outside, picked Bobbie up, opened the door, and pitched him out. Bobbie climbed the screen door, where he hung meowing piteously and staring through the glass panel in the front door. This performance angered my grandfather even more. He finally opened both doors, plucked Bobbie from the screen and pitched him into one of my grandmother's giant boxwoods below the porch.

That did it. Within a matter of minutes, I had on my mackinaw, my toboggan, and my new Christmas gloves, grabbed a chunk of cornbread from the "warming closet" of my grandmother's Home Comfort stove, filched a mayonnaise jar from the cabinet, and I was out the door. While the family (my grandparents and Uncle Asbury and Aunt Tink) gawked through the window, I crawled under the boxwood, found Bobbie, and we set out for the barn. I had decided to "run away." Bobbie and I were going to live in the barn loft.

Eventually, my grandfather trudged to the barn and stood in the feed-room calling my name. "GarNell, are you up there?"

I didn't say anything.

"What do you think you are doing?"

"Me and Bobbie are going to live over here from now on."

"You know I can't stand a cat in the house."

I didn't say anything.

"I don't have time for this foolishness. You get your little butt back to the house right now. It is going to be freezing tonight."

I didn't say anything.

"What the hell are you going to do with that mayonnaise jar?"

"Get some milk from the cow." I thought that was pretty clever. I had planned ahead.

Grandpa snorted. "You are acting like your crazy Momma."

"Maybe me and Bobbie will go live with her in Knoxville."

"We don't even know that she is there."

"Yes, you do. I heard you talking to Grandma about it."

"Come on back to the house. We are having leather britches and pintos tonight."

"Can Bobbie come too?"

Grandpa muttered something I didn't hear. Then he said, "Bring the damned cat and come on." Back at the house, I took a seat at the dinner table where Uncle Asbury and Aunt Tink sat glaring at me.

"Lord, what a aggravatin' young'en," said Aunt Tink.

"You need to blister his little bottom for him, Daddy," said Uncle Asbury. Then, he reached across the table and gave me a smack on the side of my head. "Shape up, Runt." That was his nickname for me. Then he would usually stare at me and say, "I don't see nothing of Lyndon in him." He was talking about my dead father. "I see a lot of Gilmore, though." Now he was talking about my mother who had abandoned me.

After Uncle Asbury got out of the Navy, he and Tink, his new wife, came to live with us. They got my bedroom and I had to sleep on the couch—which I didn't mind since I could listen to the big Silvertone radio. I played it real low, but Tink would sometimes come in the middle of the night and cut it off while I was listening to *Suspense* or *The Shadow*.

"We are trying to sleep!"

"Don't sound like it to me." (They made a lot of noise back there sometimes.)

"You better watch it, buster. I'm sick of you sneaking around spying on Asbury and me."

So here we sat, Bobbie and me. I was eating leather britches and pintos while everybody (except Grandma) stared at us. Grandma always stayed in the kitchen when Asbury and Tink were complaining. I got a saucer and gave Bobbie some milk. Tink was complaining about the "lack of privacy" in the house and Asbury was nodding agreement.

"Where am I supposed to go," I said.

"How about to hell," said Asbury, and laughed.

I decided to do my best imitation of the Shadow, including that great laugh he had. "What evil lurks in the hearts of men? The Shadow knows! Haa, haa, haa, haa, haa!"

"What does that mean?" said Asbury.

"Oh, it is something he gets out of those awful programs that he listens to, or them funny books he is always reading," said Grandma.

"He is already quare enough without that stuff," said Asbury.

Grandpa gave a heartfelt sigh, got up and went to stand on the back porch and stare at the Balsam Mountains. I got an old issue of *Sub-mariner* and settled on the couch. I liked Prince Namor, who lived in the depths of the ocean. He rarely visited the human cities because they were inhabited by petty, foolish humans. In this issue, Namor goes to Atlantis . . .

IN THE YEARS FOLLOWING that wintery day, I spent a lot of time with Namor or with Lamont Cranston (the Shadow) or Captain Marvel. Movies, books, and radio dramas became an escape into a world where my companions were also "outsiders." In college, my mountain dialect made me an outsider, but the movies gave me James Dean. Even now, almost seventy years after Bobbie and I fled to the barn, I still sense the subtle shift in people's attitudes when I lapse into my mountain dialect. I am outside again, and—if I close my eyes—I see Prince Namor beckoning, offering escape.

The Green Tsunami

Lonely children often take refuge in their imagination. Without playmates or distractions they may create imaginary friends and convene parliaments of comic book heroes to discuss ways to cleanse the world of evil. I know something about that. For me, in the 1940s, I often spent summer afternoons tracking Nazis and

Japanese warriors through the saw briar and broom sage behind the barn. But my favorite diversion—one that often became so real, it frightened me badly—was to create a "green tsunami."

It takes a special knack to conjure up this frightful spectacle, but I could do it. Let us say, it is a day in spring when a lush covering of vegetation is just beginning to cover the Pinnacle and Black Rock. With my grandfather off driving his Esso truck up Glenville Mountain, or down to the prison camp in Gateway, I am alone on our front porch gazing at the Balsam Mountains. Granny is in the garden and there is nothing on the radio except the *Mid-day Merry-Go-Round* from WNOX. I decide to unleash the green tsunami.

I would sit at the end of the porch facing the Balsams and give my full attention to the new foliage that had turned the entire range of peaks, coves, and hollers into varied shades of green. Then I would "squench up" my eyes. I would close my eyes tightly and then cautiously open them to tiny slits. At this point, all I could see was a great, sprawling panorama of greenery . . . a vague, pulsing expanse of shades ranging from lime to emerald to turquoise, shifting and surging . . . like a great ocean wave. What were those tiny objects that were being borne helplessly along . . . were those houses, churches, bridges? Maybe an entire town!

As I watched, I created an entire scenario. This was a tidal wave (the word "tsunami" was not yet in my vocabulary) that had traveled some 400 miles from the coast, erasing Charlotte, Greensboro, and Asheville, drowning millions and carrying the broken wreckage of factories and universities, shopping centers and malls . . . all reduced to flotsam and broken debris riding the crest of this awesome ocean tide.

By this point, I was usually so frightened that I was whimpering, and when I shut my eyes, thereby breaking my contact with the approach of an awesome flood, I turned my head and opened them again to behold the serenity of the front yard, the June apple tree and the sheltering poplars. Stretching around me was the pastures and houses of Rhodes Cove, all sleeping in the warmth of an early spring day. When I looked back at the Balsams, they had returned to their former state—a protective rampart against imaginary tsunamis. My world regained its balance and I knew with certainty that night would come, and after that, the dawn.

I once told my uncle Albert about the green tsunami. He was the only member of the family that found my fantasy life imaginative and amusing, and he would sometimes ask me, "How are things on Alpha Centauri today?" Albert was curious, and so he took a seat by me on the porch on another warm spring day. After he had learned the art of "squenching" his eyes, we were off. When we returned to the reality of Rhodes Cove, we talked about what would happen if the cataclysm we had just witnessed were real.

"What if a thousand years go by and then some archeologists dig up the wreckage of those craft shops in Cherokee?" What would they think?

"Do you think that the only people left alive in the world would be the tourist folk on Clingmans Dome and Newfound Gap?"

And so we mused, my favorite uncle and I, until it grew dark and it was time to listen to the rain crows mourn and watch the moon rise above the Balsams . . . a Yeats time, when "peace comes dropping slow."

I AM EIGHTY-EIGHT YEARS OLD now and much has happened since the green tsunamis of my youth. However, in recent years I have come to believe that the imaginary tidal wave is back . . . but it has become more complex, and very real. There are sections of the Balsams and the rest of the world around me that are no longer green . . . or at least, it is not the natural green of my youth. It is the artificial green of a golf course, or the manicured, tortured green of countless housing projects. Perhaps in an abstract sense it is the green of a greed that strives to mimic the very thing that it destroys . . . and you don't have to "squench up" your eyes to see it.

Valentino

I guess it was about 1952 when I saw the movie *Valentino* at the Ritz. As I remember it now, an athlete named Anthony Dexter had been offered a movie contract, and since he was a remarkably handsome fellow, Hollywood decided that he should portray an old movie star who had been a heartbreaker in the silent era, and—allegedly—women still visited his grave. Dexter did resemble Valentino, but the critics felt he couldn't act or dance . . . though everyone was confident that he could learn. Modern critics really trash the movie . . . but I was seventeen years old and I thought I was seeing magic. I guess I was a prime candidate to become a devoted fan, and so it was. I emerged from the Ritz like some religious fanatic. I had a hero! He had a pouty mouth and I spent hours in front of the mirror, trying to make my mouth a sensual pout. I combed my hair until my head hurt and ended up with my hair parted on both sides of my head with a big curl in the middle. Don't laugh . . . yet.

 I took my wages from working in the meat market at the A&P and I bought a pair of black pants at the Man's store. They had a pink pleat down the side that I thought was stylish, but Uncle Albert said I looked like a bellboy. Not to be deterred, I bought a white corduroy shirt. I spent hours looking at my silly face, pursing my lips and dropping my eyelids. When I thought I had it all together, I began practicing . . . the tango! I got a book out of the library that showed me the steps: one slow, another slow, and then three quicks. When my grandparents were away at the barn doing chores, I tangoed through the house, ending up in front of the mirror, where I studied my fat lips and dropped eyelids. When I had that perfected, I was ready for a public appearance.

 By this time, I had seen all of the old Valentino movies and had even ordered and read the novels that the movies were based on: *Blood and Sand*, *The Four Horsemen of the Apocalypse*.

So I felt that I knew Valentino through and through. Of course, I looked nothing like him, but in my seventeen year-old brain, I didn't know that!

THERE THEN CAME a fateful night when I went to the Teen Club which was in the old American Legion Hall, where fifty or sixty teenagers "round danced" and drank punch under the watchful eyes of two chaperones: Mrs. Buchanan, our typing teacher, and Milton Hornaday, our biology teacher. We had a sophisticated few who could do the Charleston, and some could waltz . . . but no one could tango. I had a recording of "La Cumparsita," and eventually I talked some of the girls into tangoing. It didn't go all that badly, but it wasn't a winner. I danced with Doris Moody, Joyce Nickleson and her sister Jean, a girl named Grace Davis, and one named Darla May Rice . . .

No one deliberately hurt my feelings. Several asked me what was wrong with my lip? I gradually came to understand that none of them knew who I was. I was Valentino!! Some of them had seen the movie and thought it was okay, but there were better films out there. And some of them advised me to stick to round dancing, which Albert had told me was just an excuse to "hug up and slide around." So I did that. I went back to dancing to "That's the Glory of Love" and "Harbor Lights." I guess I looked pretty silly, with my pink-pleated pants and styled hair and dropped eyelids. I enjoyed round dancing and "hugging up and sliding around." But I wanted to be Valentino, damn it!!!

I STILL WONDER ABOUT this yearning to be someone else. Later on, it would be Elvis and . . . I didn't entirely fail there. In the dark, I coast through my old house and sing Elvis hits, and—in the dark and alone—I sound pretty good.

> Love me tender, love me dear
> Tell me you are mine
> I'll be yours through all the years
> 'Till the end of time . . .

Midnight on Freeze Hill

Back in 1953, I had two wonderful friends: Darel Monteith and Ed Henson. For some years, we would drive several times each week at midnight to Keener Cemetery on Freeze Hill and park where we could see the main street of Sylva and listen to a radio program on WGN Chicago that was produced by the radio personality Franklyn MacCormic, who had a voice like warm melting honey. The program was called *Moon River* and it was a popular late-night radio show, long before *Breakfast at Tiffany's* and Andy Williams's "wider than a mile" river.

We always parked at the cemetery's highest point and the only light was the blinking caution light (the town's only traffic light in the 1950s) and listened to MacCormic recite, "Down the valley of a thousand yesterdays flow the bright, cool waters of Moon River, on and down, forever carrying you to the land of forgetfulness, the kingdom of sleep." MacCormic spoke of this river as "a place where vain desires forget themselves in the loveliness of sleep." Then, for the next thirty minutes, he read poetry while a violin whispered in the background. The poems were all romantic and sad:

> Rain fell last night . . . quiet, gentle rain
> that tapped against my window pane,
> and called me back from troubled sleep,
> to soothe a heart too numb to weep.
>
> My loneliness was too deep and real,
> and like a wound that would not heal,
> it throbbed within, and I knew,
> My arms were empty without you.
>
> But as I listened to the sound
> of soft rain falling on the ground

> I heard your voice, tender and clear,
> call my name, and oh my dear,
>
> I threw my window open wide,
> to let the sweet rain rush inside.
> It kissed my eyes, my lips, my hair,
> and love, I knew that you were there.
>
> Tears that my heart could not release
> fell down from Heaven, bringing peace.
> Last night, while gray clouds softly wept,
> I held you in my arms and slept.

When I repeat the poems that MacCormic read to us over sixty years ago, I am a bit embarrassed by them. They are what we call "schmaltz" today, but on those warm summer nights in 1953, Ed and Darel and I got all misty-eyed listening to MacCormic.

So, when *Moon River* signed off, we did our own heartfelt quotes. Over a couple of months, we had memorized a passage from Thomas Wolfe's *You Can't Go Home Again*. We had read it to each other so many times that we had developed a kind of choral recitation. First Darel would say, "Something has spoken to me in the night, burning the tapers of the waning year; something has spoken in the night, and told me I shall die, I know not where. Saying: . . ."

Then, I would quote, "To lose the earth you know, for greater knowing; to lose the life you have, for greater life; to leave the friends you loved, for greater loving . . ."

And then Ed would say, "to find a land more kind than home, more large than earth."

And then all three of us would say together the final line, "Whereon the pillars of this earth are founded, toward which the conscience of the world is tending—a wind is rising, and the rivers flow."

SO THERE WE SAT, three foolish young men, staring at that blinking caution light in the distance. Sometimes, we would drive to Fisher Creek and park near a pasture where sleepy cows regarded us, and Darel would quote Byron's "So we'll go no more a roving, so late into the night."

NOW, LOOKING BACK on those nights, I realize that we were three foolish fellows who thought we were alone in an indifferent world. None of us had the slightest idea about what Wolfe was saying . . . we just knew it was wonderful like the music that we heard from the organ on Sunday, power and meaningful, but . . . what did it mean?

The years passed and we went our separate ways. I never talked to Ed again. In the last year before he died, Darel would come and sit on my porch and we would talk. He had been a lawyer for many years and sometimes his wife would bring him to my house. Darel would go to sleep and his wife would come to wake him and lead him to the car for the long drive home to Charlotte. (He was, in fact, coming to my porch on the day that he died.) I couldn't resist my curiosity about those nights on Freeze Hill, so a couple of times while Darel and I sat in the sun on my porch, I just suddenly asked, "Do you remember Freeze Hill?"

After a moment, Darel said, "Something has spoken to me in the night . . ."

Yes, he remembered!!!

The Bootlegger's Turn

Back in 1958, around the time I graduated from Western Carolina Teacher's College, Jackson County was all atwitter about the movie *Thunder Road*, which was being shot in Asheville and Lake Toxaway. Robert Mitchum had been seen in Asheville, and rumor had it that they were buying cars to wreck. Some of my friends claimed that they had sold their cars to Mitchum just to see them go bouncing down Toxaway Falls as part of an exciting car-racing scene in which moonshiners wrecked in a desperate bid to outrun the government agents.

Oh, my! Well, like every red-blooded boy in Sylva, I wanted to see that!

We left each morning in a strange cavalcade of mismatched vehicles: family cars, pickups, and late-model Fords (Mitchum's favored wrecking choice) on our way to Toxaway Falls. So it was that I was fortunate enough to see some of the rehearsals on a road outside of Asheville in which the actors practiced the legendary "bootlegger's turn," which was allegedly practiced by moonshiners when escape seemed futile. According to my unstable friend, Ronnie Russell, the bootlegger hit the brakes and cut the wheels sharply to the left, sending his car into an immediate spin. If successfully executed, the maneuver left the driver suddenly facing the opposite direction that he had been traveling. Then, amid the stench of burning tires and smoke, he sped off, passing the astonished revenuer who was still going in the opposite direction.

Did it work? Yes, it did. In those dimly remembered rehearsals where we sat in the woods above the rehearsal road that ran along the river, it was impressive. I don't remember any scenes in the movie, which I saw too many times, but in those practice runs it left me stunned. I think there were five or six of us there, but it is Ronnie that I remember. With the fervor of the true believer in his eyes, he started practicing on the lonely midnight roads of Jackson County. Sometimes, when we were at Troy's Drive-In, I would look at Ronnie sitting on the curb. There he sat like a cocked pistol, looking for a victim. He would smirk, wink, and say, "Hey, Pilgrim. You want to see a bootlegger's turn?"

I would always shake my head and say, "No, thank ye."

Did he have takers? Oh yes. I remember Tom Ed Davis and Jimmy Stovall, who rode with Ronnie to his testing site, a mile-long stretch of road up by the old airport. When they came back, having been gone less than thirty minutes, they looked a bit pale and shaken. Tom Ed, who was known to be afraid of nothing, said, "Ronnie is crazy."

But, life went on. We all got married, moved away, became respectable, or died.

NOW, LET'S FAST FORWARD. It is 1972, and the world has been unkind to some of us. I was one. I was living in exile in Atlanta, Georgia, on Myrtle Avenue, which was noted for being occupied by those who were defeated by life. At least temporarily. I was trying to stay in Georgia long enough to get a divorce since North Carolina took two years, and I had ended up in a slum apartment with five other men from Jackson County.

I had their address on a slip of paper and when I found them, they had a single light in the kitchen, the phone had been cut off, and there was no heat. One of the occupants was a devious sneak who stole from the others, including me. The other four were reasonable fellows, all of whom I remembered from Sylva. One of them was Ronnie Russell (he was not the devious sneak). Like me, Ronnie was in the process of getting a divorce. He had made a bad marriage, but he was the father of twins and he drove to Sylva every weekend to see his sons. He was known for his laugh, which was infectious. He wore a little hat with a feather in the band, smoked constantly, and drank a case of beer each day. Eventually, I got a job in a record shop, which paid so little I could only afford two meals a day. My car had a cracked motor block, and so when Ronnie asked me if I wanted a ride to Sylva this weekend, I said yes.

I should have known better, but I had completely forgotten a lot of stuff. So on the ride from Atlanta to Sylva, Ronnie filled me in on his life. It became increasingly obvious that he was drunk. In a short time, he was weeping and rarely driving under seventy. Suddenly he said, "Gary, have you ever seen a bootlegger's turn?" Then, before I could answer, he did it.

MY FACE MERGED with the windshield and the spectral bleakness of the interstate became a smear in which night sky, pavement, moonlight and the thick, wooded hillsides all merged into a senseless mass. I felt a wave of nausea, as each item separated and became frozen in stillness. The stench of burning rubber and smoke hung in the air and I felt gravity restored. Ronnie gave his demented cackle as I fumbled for the door handle and got out. I started walking back toward Atlanta.

When Ronnie's headlights had become dim pinpoints, I saw them flare into brightness, and then I heard the engine and the tires squeal as he came down the interstate. I kept walking. He slowed to a crawl and rolled his window down.

"Come on, Gary. Let's go to Sylva."

"Tom Ed was right, Ronnie. You *are* crazy." I kept walking.

He pulled away and cut a screeching U-turn in the middle of the northbound lane. Then he came back and drove at a rate that matched my walking pace. He pulled across my path and stopped.

"Let me ask you something, Gary. What do you have to look forward to?"

I kept walking.

"Come on, I really want to know."

I found myself struggling for an answer. Finally, I said, "Well, there are some movies I really want to see."

Ronnie exploded into goat bleats of laughter. Still struggling for breath, he reached over and unlatched the door and pushed it wide. "Get in."

Finally, I did.

AFTER THAT NIGHT, when I saw Ronnie in Atlanta or in Sylva, he would say, "Some movies, huh? Name one."

"*Shane*," I would say, or "*West Side Story*."

And he would laugh that crazy laugh.

The Hoyle House

Shortly after I went to work for the Eastern Band of Cherokee Indians back in the 1980s, my wife got employment at the *Sylva Herald* and so we did the logical thing. We decided to build a house. Since my grandfather had adopted me as his son, I received a beautiful piece of land in the old pasture, and we got a local builder to build a modest house with clerestory windows in the roof and a wraparound deck. It had two stories, with one bedroom on the second floor and another on the first. I loved it from the start and some of my most pleasant memories are of lying on the floor on Sunday night, and listening to my favorite program, *Hearts of Space*. I could see the night sky through those clerestory windows as I listened to Vangelis or Hank Snow. For a decade, I was truly happy.

I WAS DELIGHTED with my three acres, and spent a great deal of time exploring the dense woods that surrounded me. There were still pheasants and quail in the woods, and when I hiked all the way to King's Mountain (there are dozens of mountains that have that name), I often found my way across the mountain and into a little cove that came to be known as Smart Carter Cove (there is a story associated with this little cove, and the man who once lived there, solitary and happy). It was a long time before I ventured down through the laurel thickets into the hillside that ended up in a section of Jackson County called Love's Field. It was there, as I made my way through a large thicket, that I found the Hoyle house.

Perhaps it is necessary to be "raised Appalachian" to understand my reaction to this rustic little house. It was a tightly constructed cottage that emerged from the hillside. There was a clean, well-kept spring in the backyard, with a tin dipper hanging on a hook, and when I drank, the water had the same taste as my grandfather's spring (yes, good water does have a distinct taste). I peeped through a back window and saw rows on rows of canned goods: corn, pickled beans, tomatoes, okra, and so on. However, it was increasingly obvious that no one was living in this house. There was a little chicken lot, but an absence of clucks and cackles. I mounted the front steps, knocked, and then tried the front door, and it opened!

It was a neatly kept home. There were two bedrooms, covered with colorful quilts, a Warm Morning stove in the living room, and a little cook stove in the kitchen. There was a little kitchen table complete with salt and pepper shakers ... It all looked as though it was waiting for someone to settle into a chair. I saw a few personal items: photographs, a calendar, and a little Philco radio. But I was becoming nervous. I had no business prowling through this house. Perhaps the people living here had simple gone to buy groceries, or visit relatives. I gently closed the front door and climbed back through the laurel thickets to my own home.

I immediately contacted a neighbor and asked about the little house. "Yes, that is the Hoyle house," he said. "I guess there is no one living there now. For years, there were two sisters and a handicapped brother, but the brother died recently. The two sisters are probably in a nursing home."

Wow! That stunned me. My mind was immediately filled with images of those three people, living in that house, sitting before that fireplace, eating those canned goods at that table, feeding those chickens. I sensed love and comfort, and I wondered if they listened to the *Grand Ole Opry* and *Renfro Valley*. I called my neighbor back and asked him what was going to become of that house.

"Well, someone should contact a relative, and I'm not sure that there are any." He called me back later. "There is a Hoyle that lives at the head of the holler here. Not a very social fellow, I'm afraid."

So I decided to find the Hoyle at the head of the holler. I made one of my rare trips into the few houses beyond Rhodes Cove. One solitary man, chopping wood in his front yard, gave

THE HOYLE HOUSE 121

me some vague information. At last, I struggled through a lot of undergrowth to find an isolated cabin. As I got closer, I found myself in a yard full of barking dogs.

When I saw the woman on the porch, I asked if I had reached the Hoyles. She shut the dogs up and came to the end of the porch and stared at me. It was not a friendly stare. Finally, she said, "You look like you need *a haircut.* Come up here on this porch and my boys and me will cut your hair for you." The enmity in her voice was almost tangible.

"No, ma'am," I managed to say. "I am looking for relatives of the Hoyle sisters who used to live near me." Silence prevailed. The woman continued to stare. "They have moved out of their house and it is vacant," I said. More silence. Then two large young men materialized behind the woman. "I thought you should know," I added lamely. "The two sisters are in a nursing home."

The woman turned and spoke to the two men, and I felt that they must be relatives. I retreated back into the dense woods, hoping that my trip had been a success. I was a bit upset by the reception that I had received, but I later learned that this family had a reputation for being unsociable.

A week later, I visited the Hoyle house again. Long before I arrived, I became anxious. Something was wrong. I discovered that the front door had been torn away and I entered to find all of the furnishings gone. The bed ticks had been carried into the woods and gutted and they were scattered through the undergrowth. Both stoves were gone and the walls were stripped of everything, including photographs. The house now had a forlorn quality that was only deepened when I found that the canned goods were smashed and the spring was full of broken Mason jars, beans, corn, and tomatoes.

The vandalized Hoyle house was my first experience with the fate that awaits all things that can no longer defend themselves. I suppose that the mattresses had been gutted in the hope that they might contain hidden money. But why destroy canned goods? Why not take them home? I had been raised to respect and honor fading traditions. There is a darkness here that is at odds with my experience, something that seeks to burn and destroy the very things that nurtured our lives.

I ONLY RETURNED to the Hoyle house once more, dreading what I would find. I had the feeling that the house was disappearing now, gently sinking into oblivion. The windows were all broken and the barren walls seem to lean inward. The floor was littered with torn clothes and the skins of animals. In one bedroom, I found one small, feral dog and a litter of pups. The room bore witness to her struggle to survive and the remains of rabbits and small animals were everywhere. She rose on trembling legs, prepared to drive me from the house, and her undernourished state was painfully evident in the outline of her ribs. What to do? I choose to do what I had done with the sullen woman who offered to cut my hair. I retreated. Out of the house . . . back through the laurels, back to a safe place that had warmth and food . . . and possibly the illusion of safety.

I DID NOT RETURN. I did not need to see the rest of that sad decline. I am sure that there is nothing there now that would speak for the honor due that quiet house and its residents that once lived there in harmony with the natural world. I am sure that progress has arrived . . . streetlights, pavement, and city water. Ah, but the Hoyle house still exists in my memory: that little spring, those Mason jars, and the waning warmth of that little kitchen.

Uncle Frank

This morning, my uncle Frank is very much on my mind. I never knew him—he was committed to the insane asylum in Morganton before I was born—but I grew up hearing talk about him. He was my grandfather's brother and each time we attended a family reunion in Cowee in Macon County, the women would gather in the kitchen at Great-Grandmother's house and whisper. They didn't just talk about Frank; they talked about a multitude of scandalous topics: babies born out of wedlock, divorces (they were just beginning to become commonplace) . . . But Frank was always a favorite topic.

What did he do that brought him to a place with bars on the windows? I asked my grandfather, who told me, "I never thought he was crazy. He was just quare." So I asked why being "quare" could get you locked up, and Grandpa said that he often wondered about that himself. "He had a bad habit of wandering off, and although he wasn't stupid, he sometimes became lost. Strangers would bring him home, and Great-Grandmother would ask them to stay for dinner and they often would. Afterwards, Frank would sit on the porch for days and say the names of places that he had been. 'Nantahala,' he would say, and then he would smile as though recalling some pleasant scene. 'Culasaja,' he would say. 'Tanasee.'"

I said that some of the places sounded like Cherokee words, and Grandpa agreed with me. Frank sometimes worked as a carpenter and he was a good one, but people would find his hammer on a plank and Frank was gone again. "Big Laurel," he would say. "Spruce Pine." "Heart's Desire" and "Land's End." He was sometimes gone for weeks, and the last time he came home talking about "Manteo" and admitted that he had seen the ocean.

Lots of folks seemed to think that Frank should be "put away," including the local preacher and the principal at the school. And so they came one day, the men in the big, black car who talked to Great-Grandmother a long time, and in the end she stood on the porch and saw her oldest son taken away . . . watched the dust settle on the wild blackberry vines. Frank looked frightened, but he went with the men in the big black car because his mother said it would be all right. Afterward, she said, "I hope I did the right thing."

NOW, THIS IS THE REASON I have been thinking about Uncle Frank, who came home thirty years later, came home to die. I have developed a yen for distant places. Yes, I watch travelogues on the TV and I lie awake in the dark and say the names of exotic places. "Stonehenge," I whisper. "Falcon's Roost." "Cleopatra's Needle." "Malvern Hill." "Stratford-on-Avon."

I wonder, is it yearning for these places that gets you in trouble, or is it actually going there? Sometimes, at night, I am awakened by the sound of a motor muttering in my driveway and I rise to peer out my window where the big, black car waits. It finally turns around and purrs back down the road.

Not yet.

Vernon Cope

Last night, I dreamed about Vernon Cope. Mr. Cope was one of my elementary school teachers, and I think he taught me math in the fourth grade. In the dream, Mr. Cope and I are fishing off of Almond Park's boat dock and we aren't catching anything, but that is okay. We just enjoy fishing, and it is a summer afternoon and we listen to the birdcalls and the wind that moves our little boat that is tied to the dock and it is just a lazy afternoon. The dream doesn't make much sense since I never went fishing with Mr. Cope, but dreams don't have much to do with the real world.

IN THE REAL WORLD, Mr. Cope was a tall, thin man who always wore a coat and tie, and he covered the big blackboard with lots of addition and subtraction. He would put 12 on the blackboard and then a minus sign and the 8, and he would turn and look at me and his eyebrows would go up and down and he would hand me the piece of chalk and I would go to the front of the room, aware that all eyes were on me, and I would draw a long line beneath the 8 and then I would print a 4 and Mr. Cope would smile and say, "Thank you, Gary," and he would wiggle his eyebrows up and down.

Mr. Cope had a joint missing in the middle finger of his right hand and he wore a gold ring on that finger that rested just below that missing joint. If we became restless and began to shift our feet and mutter while looking at the clock, Mr. Cope would tap that ring on the blackboard. Rat-a-tat-tat! Like a machine gun . . . rat-a-tat-tat-tat-tat, and total silence prevailed immediately. He would give us that searchlight stare that moved from face to face, and when he was sure he had our attention, he would go on. He would do 15 and minus 5, and then 18 minus 12 and when he had twenty unsolved problems, he would start calling names and passing out chalk until he had the whole class completing the problems. When he had corrected the laggards, he would smile, and by that time the bell would ring and we would vanish quietly into the hall, off to our next class.

Mr. Cope liked me. I know that, because he always smiled at me when I completed the problem. I wasn't an exceptional student, just a ragged little kid with bib overalls and plaid shirts. I was shy and never caused Mr. Cope to be displeased. He never rat-a-tatted his finger at me. But he surprised me at Christmas when he leaned over my desk and placed a Christmas present on my desk. Everybody else got a little sack of peppermints, but I got a present . . . a small, rectangle shape that turned out to be a pen . . . a Parker pen which was the king of pens, and I sat staring at it, stunned into silence. I looked at Mr. Cope helplessly, unable to speak. And Mr. Cope frowned slightly and briefly rested his hand on my head and said softly, "Now, Gary, where are our manners?"

Good question. I never spoke.

In time, I went on to high school and other classes and other teachers, but I never forgot my Parker pen and the fact that I carried it to every class and took hundreds of tests until it finally stopped working.

TWENTY YEARS LATER, when I was working in Cherokee, I found myself alone one afternoon in the Holiday Inn eating a mountain trout and reading a book. My book made me an odd sight in Cherokee, and Jimmy Cooper, the manager of the Holiday Inn, was fond of creating a scene by ordering me to stop reading in his restaurant, and so it was on this day, and the customers stopped eating while Jimmy lectured me.

"How many times do I have to tell you, Carden! No reading in my restaurant!!!"

And I put up my book and looked up to see Mr. Cope making his way to a table with a companion, perhaps a son. He was frail, pale, and using a cane. He settled at a table near mine and as I stood to leave, Mr. Cope smiled at me and I smiled back. As I turned to go, Mr. Cope said to his companion, "That is Gary Carden, one of my former students. He is a remarkable young man." By the time I reached my car in the parking lot, I knew what Mr. Cope said was true. I was a remarkable young man.

SEVERAL YEARS LATER, I read Mr. Cope's obituary. I am not fond of funerals, but I made a special effort to go to Moody's Funeral Home while Mr. Cope lay in what was called the Viewing Room. I saw some of Mr. Cope's former students and fellow teachers, and when I approached his casket, I noted that his hands were folded on his stomach and that gold ring was there resting just below Mr. Cope's missing finger joint. I heard a distant "Rat-a-tat-tat," and I bent down to say softly, "Mr. Cope, thank you for the Parker pen."

Yes, it had served me well.

What This House Remembers

I live in an old farmhouse that is literally falling apart. Each spring, clouds of termites rise in the bathroom and the bedroom, coating the windows and covering the kitchen stove and the mirrors in the bathroom with tiny wings—wings that clog my vacuum cleaner for weeks. In the winter, the wind howls in the eaves. It pours through the attic and flows into my bedroom like an ice-laden river. All of the doors hang off-balance, and a tennis ball, dropped in the living room, will roll slowly from room to room—like a cue ball looking for a pocket—until, eventually, it finds its way to the kitchen, coming to rest behind the sink.

But with each passing year, my affection for these canted floors and leaning walls deepens. I came to live here when I was two years old, and now, seventy years later, I still sleep in the same bedroom—the one my uncle Albert dubbed "the North Pole." The entire house bears testimony to the lives of my grandparents, and when I walk from room to room, I hear lost voices and sense fading warmth.

Just here, beneath this old flue, my grandmother tended her Home Comfort stove. And over there, on that cracked cement hearthstone that once fronted a fireplace, I used to lie whimpering on winter nights—my cheek pressed against the warm hearthstone (I was plagued with chronic earaches) while my grandmother poured warm cod liver oil from a tablespoon into my ear. There, where my computer now sets, my grandfather used to tune the old Silvertone radio and listen to *Renfro Valley* on Sunday mornings. It is also where his coffin rested, for I lived in a time in which the dead came home for a final farewell.

The old house seems to be slowly sinking into the earth, dragging with it a roofless canning house and a derelict barn. Yet there are brief moments—usually in the morning—when this dim space seems filled with a kind of tangible energy. There are mornings when I wake in the chilled air of my bedroom, sensing that I am not alone—that this empty shell has become an echo chamber. In the kitchen, my grandmother's Home Comfort radiates warmth while she conjures red-eye gravy from a black skillet. Cathead biscuits bloom in the oven and a tin coffee pot chuckles on the back burner. I feel my uncle

Albert's discontent (he suffered from migraines) as he sits leaning back in a cane-bottomed chair at the dining room table, his chair legs gouging little half-moons in the linoleum. My grandfather is milking the cow, and—any minute now—he will stomp into the kitchen with a bucket of steaming milk. From the living room comes the strains of Jo Stafford's "You Belong to Me," followed by the banter of Reed Wilson, WWNC's popular early morning DJ . . .

> Fly the ocean in a silver plane
> See the jungle when it's wet with rain.

But when my foot touches the floor, it all vanishes . . . recedes like an ocean tide withdrawing down the corridors of the years, carrying away warmth, biscuits, and my grandmother's hands through the draft of a broken window. Sometimes, I move quickly to the barren kitchen, hoping to capture a belated fragment of what was here a moment ago—perhaps the last vestiges of Albert's complaint lingers: "Ahhh, God! I didn't sleep a wink," he says, as he massages his head. And here . . . who is this towheaded creature in his peppermint striped pajamas? My God, it's me! I'm on my way to Albert's bedroom, where I will find a stack of lurid magazines beneath his pillow . . . *Captain Marvel*, *Plastic Man*, *Black Hawk*, and *The Blue Beetle*.

IS IT POSSIBLE that there are past moments that have taken refuge in these rooms? Are there moments that were fueled by such intense emotion they hang suspended like banks of summer clouds, waiting for an alignment of hours, months, and memory? My mother's grief for my father's murder is somewhere in this bedroom. My grandmother's loss of a "blue baby." The return of two sons from World War II haunts the front porch. An old, broken fiddle that played "The Waltz You Saved for Me" resonates faintly in the attic—are they all here like eavesdroppers in the next room, waiting for their cue to enter?

Perhaps a night will come when moonlight will penetrate the cobwebs on the attic window, touching the faded portrait of my father's face, and he will turn to my mother, whispering—and the two of them will laugh. Then, a dozen specters will awake causing this old house to shudder as music, heat, and the smell of red-eye gravy floats in the summer darkness. Then, children's footsteps will mingle with the slow trudge of the elderly, and blasts of snow, wind, and heat will batter these walls as spring and winter collide and this old house finally explodes leaving nothing behind but the buzz of a solitary wasp freed from its prison behind an attic window.

FINALLY, THIS OLD HOUSE will mingle with fog and moonlight, drifting through the stand of hemlocks that encircles this dim cove where my homeless spirit will rise to meet the morning sun.